W9-BZU-877

Cycling Michigan

25 OF THE BEST BIKE ROUTES IN WESTERN MICHIGAN

Other books by Karen Gentry:

Cycling Michigan: Best 30 Routes In East Michigan

Cycling Michigan

25 OF THE BEST BIKE ROUTES IN WESTERN MICHIGAN

By Karen Gentry

Production and design by Pegg Legg Publications
Maps by Michele Miller, Miller Design, Grand Rapids
Editing by Elizabeth Richar and Jim DuFresne
Cover Photo by Jim DuFresne
Inside Photography by Karen Gentry and Jim DuFresne
unless otherwise noted.

ISBN 1-882376-17-X

Printed in the United States of America

96 97 98 99   2 3 4 5 6 7 8

Thunder Bay Press

Lansing,   Michigan

To those who love to
wander outdoors in Michigan
and all who "eat to ride, ride to eat."
k.g.

25 BICYCLE TOURS IN WEST MICHIGAN

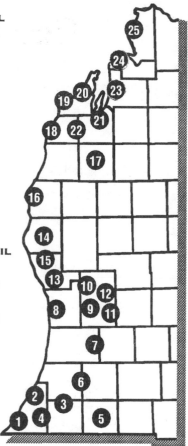

1   LAKE MICHIGAN TRAIL
2   GRAND MERE DUNES
3   SISTER LAKES
4   BLOSSOMLAND
5   AMISH TOUR
6   KAL-HAVEN TRAIL
7   SAUGATUCK TOUR
8   DUTCH DELIGHT
9   KENT TRAILS
10 APPLE COUNTRY
11 FALLASBURG FUN
12 SQUIRES STREET
13 BLOCKHOUSE HILL
14 SILVER LAKE AMBLE
15 HART-MONTAGUE TRAIL
16 NORDHOUSE DUNES
17 LAKE CADILLAC LOOP
18 CRYSTAL LAKE
19 SLEEPING BEAR TOUR
20 LAKE LEELANAU
21 OLD MISSION TOUR
22 BEETHOVEN AMBLE
23 TRIP AROUND TORCH
24 HEMINGWAY TOUR
25 TUNNEL OF TREES

KEY TO MAP SYMBOLS

Restrooms

Food Market

Restaurant

Camping

Lodging

Bike Shop

Park

Shopping

Picnic Spot

Contents

Introduction

25 Bicycle Tours

Southwest Michigan

Central West Michigan

Northwest Michigan

Appendix

Acknowledgments

I've always liked the exhilaration of exercising outdoors. I used to jog outdoors for exercise and fitness but several years ago, a couple of friends of mine convinced me to buy a new bicycle and then invited me on cycling trips. (Thanks, Joan and Gordon!) Since then I've thoroughly enjoyed the camaraderie and the fun of cycling, whether in a large group, with a few friends, or by myself. It's always a grand adventure getting to know people through cycling, discovering new roads or paths, locating a new place to eat or shop and learning the backroads of our West Michigan region.

The idea for this book originated when my friend Joan, an unabashed cycling enthusiast, designed a route in my hometown of St. Joseph/Benton Harbor. We cycled that route a couple of times, in spring and fall, and decided to write an article about it. Later when I was given the opportunity to write a book on bike routes in West Michigan, I was amazed at the excitement and interest that the idea generated. I am deeply grateful to the many friends and family members who supported me on this project.

First of all, I would like to thank all those who cycled with me, helped me map out the routes or offered moral support including Joan, Gordon, Steph, Ann, Tim, Bill, Mary, Jean, Bernice, Cindy, Glennda, Chris and Julie. I appreciate the help from Diane Ruggles from St. Joseph County and June Thaden and other members of the Cherry Capital Cycling Club. A special thanks to Tony for his help with the Sister Lakes and Torch Lake routes. An award should go to Kathy for putting up with me for a week in northwest Michigan. She helped immensely with her knowledge, good-natured humor and ability to read maps, not to mention her enthusiasm for travel and the outdoors. I am grateful to my parents for their love and encouragement. Thanks to my dad for the use of his computer - a real lifesaver - and to my sister, Jane for her computer assistance. I would also like to thank all the people I met along the way and the help from many visitors bureaus throughout West Michigan. I am grateful to Jim DuFresne and Bill Bailey from Glovebox Guidebooks for their contagious enthusiasm for travel in Michigan and their ongoing support of this project.

Lastly, I want to thank Libby Richart, who wholeheartedly jumped in on this project. She became a little sick of reading about "tunnels of trees", but she stuck with it. I appreciate her creative talents and all the time and hard work she put into editing this book.

k.q.

SAFETY AND RESPONSIBILITY

Safety is an important concern in all outdoor activities. No guidebook can alert you to every hazard or anticipate the cycling ability of every reader. Therefore, the descriptions of roads and routes in this book are not representations that a particular excursion or tour will be safe for your party. When you follow any route described in this book, you assume responsibility for your own safety. Under normal conditions, such tours require the usual attention to traffic, road and trail conditions, weather, the endurance level of your party, and other factors.

GLOVEBOX GUIDEBOOKS

A cyclist pauses along a wooded stretch in the Sleeping Bear Dunes

Introduction

WHY WEST MICHIGAN?

Besides being just darn good exercise, there are three reasons why I cycle. Food probably tops the list. In my cycling crowd, what food to pack and where to stop to enjoy it is an ever popular topic of conversation. Nothing better justifies chowing down then first biking 10, 30 or even 50 miles.

But the second reason occurred to me one afternoon in late September when I was cycling in northwest Michigan, enjoying the crisp air and the warm sunshine. Riding along at a good pace, I slowed down to admire the river up ahead where the trees had just started to change colors forcing me to take a break.

I pulled over on the bridge and watched the flowing river, felt the gentle breezes and reflected how thankful I was for days like these. As I gazed on the water, I was struck by the beauty and simplicity of the scene. Because of this spot and numerous others in West Michigan, I know why people love to bicycle in this special region.

It could be a gurgling trout stream, a shimmering inland lake, or windswept dunes along Lake Michigan. It could be wildflowers interspersed between rocks, a dense section of hardwood trees, or the smell of apple blossoms. It might be careening down a hill with a panoramic valley and farmland off into the distance or the delight of cycling on a straight, flat, newly asphalt bike path. These are the moments that make cycling so special. Although I'm a little partial, West Michigan can give you more moments like these than any other region in the state and maybe even the Midwest.

The third reason can be summed up by my eight-year-old nephew.

"I want to go with you. My feet might hurt, but I don't care." said Patrick, when he heard about a bike trip I was planning with his parents. A 20-mile loop with hills, cycling over a highway...nah, he's not ready yet. Maybe a stretch of the flat Hart-Montague Trail, perhaps the route around Lake Cadillac - he could handle that.

Patrick's reaction to this particular outing was just another enthusiastic response I received from many people when they found out I was writing this book. All kinds of people of all ages are cycling enthusiasts. Cycling is a recreational sport that fills the urge to be outdoors and to be active, to travel and to explore. Excitement and support from family and friends is definitely what kept me going and kept me inspired to explore the best routes in Western Michigan while writing this book.

Good eating, great scenery and enthusiastic friends to share it all with. What could possibly be better than that?

WHY WEST MICHIGAN?

For this book, West Michigan is defined as the western half of the Lower Peninsula, from Berrien, Cass and St. Joseph counties along the Indiana border to Emmet County on the Straits of Mackinac, to the eastern shore of Lake Michigan (sometimes confusing for you Chicagoans!). The 25 routes in this book range from the southwest corner of the state by New Buffalo to Cross Village in northwest Michigan and include inland areas such as Kalamazoo, Grand Rapids and Cadillac.

West Michigan is blessed with a 1,000 miles of Lake Michigan shoreline, the world's greatest collection of freshwater dunes, hundreds of inland lakes, rivers and streams and endless acres of forests. This scenic, natural beauty is complemented by delightful towns and attractions as well as friendly folks intent on making your stay here a pleasant one.

West Michigan's history is steeped in stories of Indians, French explorers, a lumbering era and a rich agricultural tradition. Many

Great Lake views are common along many West Michigan bike tours.

towns are named after our first residents, the Indians; Kalamazoo, Paw Paw, Manistee and Muskegon are but a few. Many West Michigan communities then prospered in the lumbering era. After the Civil War, Michigan emerged as one of the leading lumber-producing regions in the country. The first sawmill in West Michigan was built in 1836 in Grand Rapids, followed by another in Muskegon in 1860. Soon mills were built at the mouths of most rivers emptying into Lake Michigan.

Later, the emphasis shifted from rivers to railroads to a system of highways and roadways with the emergence of the automobile. That lead to the region's long history of tourism and its eventual name, "Michigan's Gold Coast." The dunes, the beautiful beaches

15

and those golden sunsets melting into the endless blue of Lake Michigan charmed visitors from the days when steamships and ferry boats were crossing over Lake Michigan from Chicago and Milwaukee. Today, they arrive by car, with their bicycles strapped on top, but they are still looking for many of the same attractions; dunes, beautiful beaches and glorious sunsets.

By cycling the routes in this book, the history of the region comes alive through rail trails, museums, Centennial farms, lumber baron mansions, covered bridges and century old summer homes. Cycling is an excellent way to find hidden corners and to learn about Michigan's colorful past.

THE ROUTES

This book describes routes, ranging from 4 to 55 miles, highlighting 25 West Michigan areas. It is geared for cyclists of all abilities, with an emphasis on day excursions and cycle touring. Routes can easily be lengthened or combined for a weekend of cycling or even longer. On most of the routes, 10- or 12-speed touring bicycles are recommended. But mountain or hybrid bicycles can be used and are even recommended on the Kal-Haven Trail and the St. Joseph County route. The routes are a mixture of narrow roads with no shoulders, busy roadways with paved shoulders and bike paths through towns, woods, forests and open farm country. Most important, the tours are geared for sightseeing, and eating, not competitive racing. Shorter options are ideal for beginners or those that don't want to go a long distance.

The West Michigan region has been divided into three sections: Southwest, Central West and Northwest. Most of the routes list attractions that will be of interest to cyclists such as places to stop and eat, creative lodging ideas and bicycle shops in the area. The route descriptions and directions will give you an idea of the terrain while covering the unique aspects of each trip. Three of the routes (Kal-Haven, Hart-Montague and Kent Trails) are partially on converted rail beds, part of the growing rails-to-trails movement (see appendix).

A cyclist crosses a covered bridge, one of several in West Michigan.

To develop the tours, I consulted bicycling clubs, studied state and county cycling maps and worked with local tourism officials before hitting the road and riding the routes. These are by no means the only cycling routes worth touring in West Michigan - we could probably provide you with 100 tours. But these are some of the very best and provide an excellent taste of our beautiful region.

CLIMATE

Changeable is the word that best describes weather in West Michigan. Although some cyclists chase their sport year-round, May through October are the most popular months to cycle in West Michigan. In May, even earlier in April, showers are frequent but there are also pleasant stretches of weather when the skies are blue and temperatures are a comfortable 50 to 60 degrees. Wildflowers are emerging along roadsides at this time of year and best of all there's no bugs to stick to your teeth.

There is more traffic in West Michigan June through August, due to the region's popularity as a vacation designation. Temperatures at this time of year can range anywhere from a pleasant 70 degrees to a blistering 90 degrees. Sunny weather and clear skies are the norm but watch for sudden thunderstorms that rumble off Lake Michigan and across the state.

If you can get away, fall is an ideal time to cycle in West Michigan. From September through October temperatures return to those pleasant levels below 70 degrees. Showers are common (especially on the weekends it seems) but so are those glorious Indian summer days when the sky is azure blue, the air dry and the trees are peaking in their autumn hues of red, yellow and vivid orange. The hardwoods in West Michigan begin changing colors in mid-September and peak from the first week of October in areas around Petoskey, to the end of that month at the southwest corner.

Riding after October? Just make sure you wear your wool gloves and long underwear. Regardless when you ride, always pack rain gear or at least a windbreaker, even if the sun is shining when you begin. You never know with Michigan weather!

BICYCLE SAFETY

Bicycle helmets are strongly recommended whenever you go riding. Wearing a helmet can prevent serious head injuries and reduces (some experts say by as much as 85 percent) the chances of injuring yourself if you are thrown from your bicycle. Look for the Snell or ANSI sticker on the inside of the helmet. Although helmets can be expensive, they are a necessary investment for all cyclists.

Here are some other tips for a safe trip:

Safety check your bike: Before a tour, especially a long one, perform a quick inspection of your bicycle, paying close attention to your brakes, spokes, tires and quick release hubs. Make sure

Various children's seats and carriers make biking a family activity.

everything is operating smoothly to avoid an unexpected mishap on the road.

Ride with the flow of traffic: Do not ride against the flow of traffic and do not pull off the road every time a car approaches on narrow shoulders. Be careful: the transition between roadbed and shoulder is rarely smooth and can cause you to lose control.

Increase your visibility: Wear bright colored clothes and jackets instead of darker colors or earth tones to increase your visibility with motorists.

Pay attention to the road: There is a tendency at times to daydream while cycling long distances. It's easy to do as you fall into a rhythmic trance due to the constant motion of pedaling. But be alert for road signs, intersections, and patches of loose gravel, wet leaves or unexpected pot holes.

Observe all traffic signs: More times than not cycling accidents are caused by careless cyclists. Avoid coasting through stop signs or racing through yellow lights. Treat every intersection as if you were in a car.

Be prepared for bothersome dogs: Some bikers carry a spray can of dog repellent that can be purchased at any good bike shop. Others simply try to "outrun" the dog. Whatever, have a plan ready for when a snapping mutt is chasing you.

PACKING FOR A BIKE TOUR

Always bring plenty of water. If there is any room in your bike bags after you've packed the other necessities (a dozen Hershey bars, boxes of fruit juice, a pound of trail mix, ect.) you might want to throw in a few tools. The four most common bike breakdowns on the roads are flat tires, broken brake cable, a suddenly wobbling wheel and an off-sprocket chain.

All four can be repaired at roadside if you have the right tools. At this point the Hershey bars are useless. Here's a list of suggested tools. Pack what the distance and number of days you'll be on the road dictate:

Crescent wrench: Don't ride anywhere without one. Useful to change a tire, adjust spokes and tighten any nut or bolt that comes loose.

Tire irons: Three plastic ones are lightweight and make changing a tire a lot easier.

Tube patch kit: Along with the kit, you should pack along a spare tube on longer rides.

Frame-mounted tire pump: How else are you going to inflate the spare or add some extra air to your tires?

Screwdrivers: Both a slot and a Phillips head type. Your best bet is to invest in a small tool kit from a bike shop designed to provide what you need when repairing your bike on the road or be easily stored in a compact case when you're not.

Small can of WD-40: It's nice to carry some lubrication along on those multi-day bike tours.

This and that: Depending on your bike model, you might want Allen wrenches, vise grip pliers and paper clips when all else fails. It's amazing what you can repair with a paper clip.

One more thing; either know how to make the necessary repairs, pack along the manual or ride with a friend who can. All the tools in the world are useless if you don't know what you're doing. In which case the dozen Hershey bars comes in handy...gives you something to do while waiting for help.

KAREN'S FAVORITES:

Every route in this book is special in its own way. To have some fun, I came up with these categories to serve as a further guide.

Most romantic: Saugatuck shorter option.

Best for kids: Hart-Montague Trail.

Best for large groups: Hart-Montague Trail.

Best workout for experienced cyclists: Sleeping Bear/ Glen Lake.

Most scenic: Old Mission Peninsula.

Best lakeshore route: Ludington.

Best wooded inland: Kal-Haven Trail.

And finally the best gastronomical tour on a bicycle: Geez, I don't know, you can eat well on all of them...but the Torch Lake tour does wind past the best ice cream shops and eateries.

Happy Cycling!!!

A Backroads Bikeway sign that marks the Lake Michigan Trail.

1 Lake Michigan Trail

TRIP CARD
Starting point: Three Oaks
County: Berrien
Distance: 31 miles
Shorter option: 8 miles
Terrain: mostly flat, some rolling hills
Highlights: Bicycle Museum, New Buffalo,
Lake Michigan, Warren Woods Natural Area
Suggested riders: beginners to intermediate

Picture a small town in southwestern Michigan, near the Indiana border. It's a small town of under 2,000 residents; a quiet, pleasant community with an annual Flag Day Festival in June. Then, picture this same town with 7,000 cyclists converging on the area for the annual Apple Cider Century, happening at the end of September every year.

That's what you have in Three Oaks, Michigan, located 10 miles inland from Lake Michigan, five miles from the Indiana border and 20 miles from the St. Joseph/Benton Harbor area in southwestern Michigan. The Apple Cider Century is a one-day event, offering cyclists a choice of 25, 50, 75 or 100-mile rides through a variety of scenery; orchards, woods, vineyards, wineries, the Lake Michigan shoreline and pleasing small towns.

Since that rainy, cold day of the first Apple Cider Century in 1974, the event has grown to become the Midwest's biggest one-day century event. The annual event is sponsored by the Three Oaks Spokes Bicycle Club, a group of cycling enthusiasts from Indiana and Michigan. The Three Oaks area would have to be the bicycling mecca of West Michigan if one were named. Monies raised from the Apple Cider Century supports the popular Bicycle History Museum, located on Elm Street in downtown Three Oaks, and for signs and four-color brochures for the Backroads Bikeway, a system of 10 self-guided routes in the area. All the routes in the brochure, ranging from 8-60 miles, begin at the Bicycle Museum. The routes are easy to follow with the brochure, and because of the green and white Backroads Bikeway signs throughout the system.

Bryan Volstorf, executive director of the museum, works year round to make sure the annual Apple Cider Century goes off without a hitch. The museum averages 8,000 to 10,000 visitors per year, not counting the visitors on the one-day Apple Cider Century. Cyclists will enjoy Michigan's only Bicycle Museum, with its collection of bicycles from the 1860's to the present. On display are the Boneshaker, a 1870's model which literally shook bones on those dirt roads, a highwheeler, a wooden spoked bicycle, a chainless bicycle from 1890, balloon tire bicycles to modern day models.

A variety of commemorative T-shirts and cycling accessories are also for sale at the museum and there's lots of free West Michigan travel information.

The Backroads Bikeway routes follow gurgling streams, open farm country, two state parks, Lake Michigan shoreline and numerous shady, wooded roads and farm markets. The routes in this and the next chapter were taken largely from the tours listed in the Backroads Bikeway brochure and adapted for the book.

The 31-mile circuit and the shorter 8-mile option head south out of Three Oaks. The longer loop heads south from the Bicycle Museum and west toward Lake Michigan, into the town of New Buffalo - a lakeside, resort community filled with dockominiums, condominiums, antique shops, restaurants and bars. It's a tourist town, especially popular with Chicagoans; New Buffalo is the first Michigan town along the big lake.

This route takes you through the Warren Woods Nautral

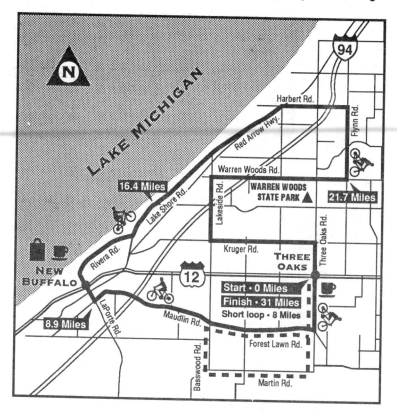

Area, a nice place to take a break and walk on the trails. The shorter 8-mile loop will give beginning cyclists a chance to see some of the countryside while their more adventurous friends and family members go for the distance.

Stage one (8.9 miles) Head south on Elm Street out of the town of Three Oaks. You will pass a couple of family restaurants as you cycle through downtown Three Oaks. Drier's Butcher Shop, on the right, is an old-fashioned butcher shop, a historic site in a centennial building that some say features the best homemade liverwurst in the Midwest. In less than a mile you will be in open country. Turn right on Forest Lawn Road at 1.8 miles to reach the

Historic Drier's Butcher Shop in Three Oaks.

Forest Lawn Cemetery-large, hilly and scenic- at 2.3 miles. The road twists and turns as you make your way to New Buffalo and a stately row of hardwoods is passed at 4.8 miles. The road then curves and becomes Maudlin Road. More twists, more trees. There's a nice shady area at 7.1 miles while at 8.9 miles you will be in front of an interesting attraction, The New Buffalo Railroad Museum and The Roundhouse at 530 S. Whittaker Street. The museum includes local history and railroad memorabilia from the Pere Marquette, Michigan Central, C&P, Chessie and Amtrak lines. The Roundhouse is in the renovated Pere Marquette Railway Roundhouse and features upscale shops, great antiques and crafts.

Stage two (10.8 miles) From Maudlin Road, turn (north) right on Whittaker Street into downtown New Buffalo. Hungry?? There's plenty of places to eat here such as Shelly's Yogurt Parlour, Casey's Pub, Rosie's Restaurant, Burhap's Crab House. Turn right on Rivera Road, hugging the lakeshore to Lake Shore Road (Rivera Road ends at Lake Shore Road). From Lake Shore Road turn left on Red Arrow Highway at 16.4 miles where you'll pass a Backroads Bikeway sign to help point you in the right direction. Red Arrow Highway has some interesting options for a break including an antique mall, Capozios Pizza at 16.9 miles and the Honeycutt Market, on the right at 17.1 miles. You'll pass through the village of Harbert at 17.3 miles (don't blink or you'll miss it!). Turn right on Harbert Road at 17.5 miles, cross Three Oaks Road and then turn right on Flynn Road at 19.7 miles.

Stage three: (10.9 miles) Flynn Road is a narrow country road. A hilly stretch is reached at 20.4 miles followed by a canopy of trees and then open country at 21.5 miles. Turn right on Warren Woods Road at 21.7 miles. B&J Country Store is on the corner of Three Oaks Road and Warren Woods Road, a good place for pop or a candy bar. A long hill follows as the route curves to the right at 23.4 miles and travels through the Warren Woods Natural Area. Bob-A-Ron Campground, with 190 modern sites and 125 primitive sites, is on your left at 24.3 miles. Turn left on Lakeside Road at 25.8

Bryan Volstorf, director of the Three Oaks Spokes Bicycle Museum, a delightful stop for any cyclist.

miles and within a half mile you pass over I-94. At 26.7 miles turn left on Kruger Road, a level road through open countryside. Turn right on Three Oaks Road at 30.6 miles and in a short jaunt you'll be back at the Bicycle Museum and the starting point.

Shorter option (8 miles) From the Bicycle Museum, head south on Elm Street (Three Oaks Road) to Forest Lawn Road; turn right. Travel Forest Lawn Road to Basswood Road and turn left (south). Ride to Martin Road; turn left (east). Take Martin Road back to Three Oaks Road. Turn left here and head into downtown Three Oaks and back to your starting point at the Bicycle Museum.

Bicycle sales, service

Cycle Path, 5684 St. Joseph Ave., Stevensville; (616) 429-4483.

Baker's Bike Shop Inc., 135 Dixie Way S., South Bend, IN; (219) 277-8866.

Bike Specialists, 603 N. 2nd St., Niles; (616) 683-3100.

Area events and festivals

June: Flag Day Festival, Three Oaks.

September: Apple Cider Century, Three Oaks; Four Flags Area Apple Festival, Niles.

Area attractions

The Roundhouse, New Buffalo; (616)469-3166

The New Buffalo Railroad Museum, New Buffalo; (616)469-3166 or (616)469-3839

Fernwood Nature Center, Niles; (616) 695-6491

Tabor Hill Winery & Restaurant, Buchanan; (800)283-3363

Cook Energy Information Center, Bridgman; (616) 465-5144 or (800) 548-2555.

Travel information

Backroads Bikeway, 110 N. Elm St., Three Oaks, MI 49128; (616) 756-3361 (SASE for free Backroads Bikeway brochure).

Harbor Country Chamber of Commerce, New Buffalo; (616) 469-5409.

Michigan Travel Information Center, New Buffalo; (616)469-0011.

Four Flags Area Council on Tourism, Niles; (616)683-8870

Southwestern Michigan Tourist Council, Benton Harbor; (616) 925-6301.

The Lake Michigan beach at Grand Mere State Park.

2 Grand Mere Dunes

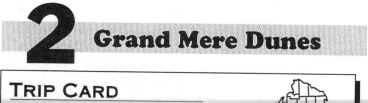

TRIP CARD

Starting point: Grand Mere State Park
County: Berrien
Distance: 50 miles
Shorter option: 17 miles
Terrain: mostly flat, some rolling hills
Highlights: Grand Mere and Warren Dunes State Park, Warren Woods , Bicycle Museum, vineyards
Suggested riders: intermediate, beginners for shorter loop

Grand Mere was designated a state park in 1973, but it wasn't until the 1990's that a portion of the park's master plan was implemented. It used to be an area known only by locals and residents who summered there, including Chicago celebrities, with many wanting the dunes and three small lakes to remain a well-kept secret. Slowly the rest of the state is discovering the lakeshore beauty of Grand Mere.

The park features a shelter, hiking trails, sand dunes, varied land formations and flora, not to mention an easily accessible parking area, which makes it a good starting point for this 50-mile route. Most of all, Grand Mere is blessed with a beautiful, wide sandy beach on Lake Michigan, an ideal place to cool off after any bike tour in the summer. Grand Mere is also only 7 miles from downtown St. Joseph, which offers an array of shopping, a kids' museum, art center and numerous restaurants.

These two routes were adapted from the Backroads Bikeway brochure, developed by the Three Oaks Spokes Bicycle Club. The

31

longer route begins at Grand Mere State Park, near Stevensville, a bedroom community to the St. Joseph and Benton Harbor area.

From Grand Mere, the ride heads south toward the better known and more developed Warren Dunes State Park, that features a large modern campground as well as an impressive beach of its own. This 50-mile circuit then makes its way toward Three Oaks, traveling past Warren Woods Natural Area, open farmland and then through downtown Three Oaks, the only town in Michigan with a Bicycle Museum (see tour 1). The terrain on this route is varied enough to delight most cyclists and includes wide open roads, stretches of shaded pavement and a couple of small towns. Baroda is "Smalltown, U.S.A.", little more than a "V" shaped intersection, 1,000 residents, and a few places to eat (or drink!) that attracts more than just those who call Baroda home.

The 50-mile route and the 17-mile shorter option offer cyclists variety with a capital "V". Where else could you find Lake Michigan shoreline, two state parks, lush farmfields, vineyards, a bicycle museum and a century old butcher shop (downtown Three Oaks) that appears to have changed little since opening in 1875.

Stage one (16.6 miles) From the entrance of Grand Mere, head south on Thornton Road as it curves and winds past the forested state park. In 2.8 miles, you'll reach Livingston Road where you turn left and cross Red Arrow Highway. Caution: Red Arrow can be busy in the summer and fall. At 3.8 miles turn right on Jericho Road, a level ride through scenic, open country. You'll pass Lemon Creek Road and the Pebblewood Country Club and Golf Course and at Snow Road you've pedalled 7.1 miles. Turn right.

Snow Road makes a couple of curves in the next two miles, the second time while you're heading downhill. At 10.5 miles, turn right on Browntown Road, and then turn left on Flynn Road a mile later. You'll struggle up a steep hill at 12 miles and then pass a picturesque church on the corner of Flynn and Sawyer roads within a half mile. Flynn becomes somewhat bumpy at 13.3 miles, then turns into a delightful downhill stretch through a shady area followed by an

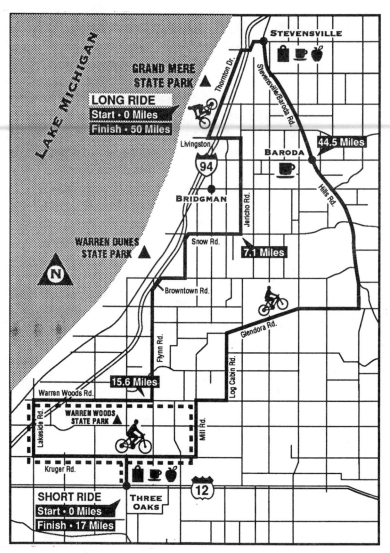

uphill ride through a canopy of trees at 14.2 miles. At Flynn and Warren Woods Road, you've gone 15.6 miles; turn right on Warren Woods Road. Time for your first break or a candy bar Both from B&J Country Store on the corner of Warren Woods Road and Three Oaks Road at 16.6 miles.

Stage two (8.9 miles) From B&J Country Store, continue heading west (left) on Warren Woods Road. In less than a mile, you'll be cycling through the Warren Woods Natural Area and past a posted trailhead. This 300-acre preserve is actually a part of Warren Dunes State Park and represents one of the last virgin climax beech-maple forests in the state. The trail is a 2-mile loop to the Galien River. Even if that's too much hiking on your day to bike, just wander a hundred yards down the wooded path and you'll see virgin beech so large that two people can't link their arms around them. This gorgeous, wooded shade is great for a weather-beaten cyclist sizzled by a hot August afternoon.

Warren Woods Road curves a bit to the right as you leave the natural area and head into a residential section. At 18.2 miles, the Bob-A-Ron Campground is on your left (canoeing, fishing, swimming, plus modern and primitive sites). From there it's uphill and over I-94 where below you will be the summer snarl of travelers rushing off to their "vacation," and at 19.7 miles you turn left on Lakeside Road, a road that's narrow, but well shaded. Lakeside also involves a couple of long uphill climbs before you turn left on Kruger Road at 21.5 miles. After a stretch of scenic rolling farm fields, turn right on Three Oaks Road at 24.5 miles and look south for Three Oaks' skyline in the distance. You won't see one because this homey village of of less than 2,000 doesn't have one. What it does have, appearing soon on your left, is the world famous (okay, how about Midwest famous) Bicycle Museum (see tour 1) at 25.3 miles. The museum is in the south end of downtown Three Oaks, where there are several options for a short or longer rest. The museum itself has picnic tables for cyclists or there's a couple of family restaurants, historic Drier's Butcher Shop, a gas station/convenience store for a smorgasbord of junk food, and Roma Pizza on your left at 25.5 miles.

Stage three (19 miles) From downtown Three Oaks, backtrack by heading north on Three Oaks Road to Kruger Road; turn right. Kruger Road is a road with picturesque farmland typical

The trailhead at Warren Woods Natural Area.

of this rural corner of the state. At 29.1 miles, turn left on Mill Road and cycle 2 miles to Warren Woods Road; turn right. Travel east for a mile, cross the Galien River and then immediately turn left onto Log Cabin Road, a narrow road that features a one-lane bridge. At 34.4 miles turn right on Glendora Road where you cycle pass the seen-better-days Lintner Tavern, a white clapboard structure, before entering the hamlet of Glendora. After a couple of rolling hills, turn left (north) on Hills Road, which is a slightly bumpy but shaded roadway. Smell the air, and savor the aroma as you cycle through vineyards at 40.3 miles. A long hill is encountered at 41.5 miles and then the road curves sharply to the right and you'll pass Heart of the Vineyard Bed & Breakfast (616-422-1617) at 42 miles.

In less than a half mile from the bed and breakfast, Hills Road merges into Snow Road and then immediately veers to the right (and later becomes Stevensville/Baroda Road). Stay on Hill Road and at 43.6 miles you'll pass an arrow pointing to Lemon Creek Winery and Fruit Farms (616-471-1321), a family-owned vineyard, offering winery tours and opportunities to pick fruit in season from their orchards. At 44.5 miles you'll arrive at Baroda, a Centennial community with a population of only 657. Baroda is rural Americana, with red, white and blue banners waving to you as you ride through town. Need a break? You will soon pass on your left Connie's Place and Bill's Tap, two bar/restaurants.

Stage four (5.8 miles) The last part of the journey leads out of Baroda and heads toward Stevensville. Continue cycling on Stevensville-Baroda Road and after 46 miles you'll cross Cleveland Avenue, a very busy four-way intersection. There's a "Welcome to Stevensville" sign at 48.9 miles and within a half mile, you'll be in downtown Stevensville, a small lakeshore community. Here Stevensville-Baroda Road becomes St. Joseph Avenue and you turn left on John Beers Road to head west toward Lake Michigan. Cycle Path Bike Shop is located in downtown Stevensville. Cross Red Arrow Highway, a busy intersection at 49.8 miles, and at this point

John Beers Road turns into a long, downhill stretch. Careful: the road curves to the right and you will still need to watch for cars on this lightly traveled road as you careen down the steep hill. Turn left on Thornton Drive and at 50.3 miles, you're back to the entrance to Grand Mere State Park. Relax, it's time to stretch those legs, look for rare plants, do dune climbing or just spread out on the beach and recuperate.

Shorter option (17 miles) From Bicycle Museum in downtown Three Oaks, head north on Three Oaks Road to Kruger Road; turn right. Cycle on Kruger Road to Mill Road; turn left (north). Follow the Backroads Bikeway signs. Turn left on Warren Woods Road through Warren Woods Natural Area to Lakeside Road. Turn left (south) on Lakeside, back to Kruger Road and turn left (east). Travel east on Kruger Road to Three Oaks Road where you turn right (south) and return to the Bicycle Museum.

Bicycle repair, sales
Cycle Path, 5684 St. Joseph, Stevensville; (616) 429-4483.
Wegner's Schwinn Cyclery, 2621 Niles Ave., St. Joseph; (616) 983-2453.

Area attractions
Bicycle Museum, 110 N. Elm St., Three Oaks; (616) 756-3361.
Lemon Creek Winery, Berrien Springs, (616) 471-1321.
Cook Energy Information Center, Bridgman; (616) 465-5144 or (800) 548-2555

Area events and festivals
June: Flag Day, Three Oaks.
July: Discover Stevensville Festival, Stevensville.
Late September: Apple Cider Century, Three Oaks.

Travel information
Southwestern Michigan Tourist Council, Benton Harbor; (616) 925-6301

Harbor Country Chamber of Commerce, New Buffalo; (616) 469-5409.

Watery views are the highlight of the Sister Lakes tour.

3 Sister Lakes

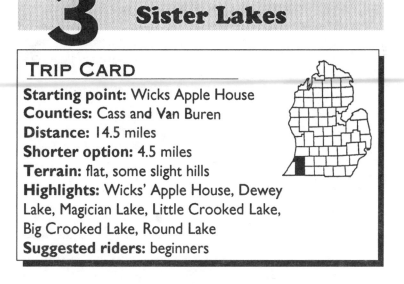

TRIP CARD

Starting point: Wicks Apple House
Counties: Cass and Van Buren
Distance: 14.5 miles
Shorter option: 4.5 miles
Terrain: flat, some slight hills
Highlights: Wicks' Apple House, Dewey Lake, Magician Lake, Little Crooked Lake, Big Crooked Lake, Round Lake
Suggested riders: beginners

The first thing cyclists need to know about this loop is that Sister Lakes doesn't exist. That is, Sister Lakes is not a body of water, but a town, situated near a series of six lakes. This 14.5-mile bicycle route ambles around these lakes in a tour that touches two southwestern Michigan counties - Van Buren and Cass - while being very close to Berrien County. It's a short circuit that starts at Wicks' Apple House, a relaxing restaurant with great lunches and a produce market, bakery and cider mill. The best season for this route is the fall to enjoy what Wicks has to offer and to see the harvest and the autumn palette of colors reflected in the waters of this easily accessible region.

Sister Lakes is a mere 90 miles from Chicago, and 30 miles from South Bend, Indiana. It's also convenient to the St. Joseph/Benton Harbor area and Kalamazoo in southwestern Michigan. The resort area has attracted visitors since 1876 when Nelson Decker opened a blacksmith shop and made an all-day horse and buggy trip to Benton Harbor to meet the ferry from Chicago. Crooked Lake, one of the six lakes, even had an excursion steamboat operating until 1903.

Today the Sister Lakes area is a low-key resort area, with unpretentious cottages and resorts featuring small cabins on the lakes. In summer, there's lots of boating and swimming on the water, probably because these lakes are warmer than Lake Michigan.

This route could easily be combined with the Three Oaks Backroads Bikeway routes, described earlier, for a weekend outing. The loop winds around several of the lakes in this area and at one point you cycle between two lakes, the 110-acre Big Crooked Lake and the 103-acre Little Crooked Lake. This stretch provides the unusual ride of gliding past the two bodies of water as if you were on a bridge.

The Sister Lakes tour also includes the Sacred Heart of Mary Catholic Church, an old mission church with an equally interesting cemetery featuring gravestones dating back to the mid-1800's. This scenic country church is a Michigan historic site and attracts so many vacationers during the summer that an outdoor pavilion was built.

There are several small-town places to eat. Try the Driftwood Summer Shop (616-424-3342) near Sister Lakes for hand-dipped ice creams (including my favorite, Mackinac Island Fudge!) or the Country Corner Coffee Shop and Frosty Delight in town. Four miles from Wicks' Apple House, is another orchard stop, Tree-Mendus Fruit Farm (616-782-7101), on Eureka Road in Eau Claire. Owners Herb and Liz Teichman know how to make families and large groups feel welcome with shaded picnic areas, restrooms, orchard tours and sun-ripened fruits in season. In July, the fruit farm conducts the annual Cherry Pit Spitting competition that attracts contestants from all over the country. Patooey!

Stage one (9.5 miles) From Wicks' Apple House, cycle north on Indian Lake Road and then turn right on Topash Street in 0.3 mile. The road is narrow and lightly travelled and passes vineyards, cornfields and red raspberry farms within the first mile.

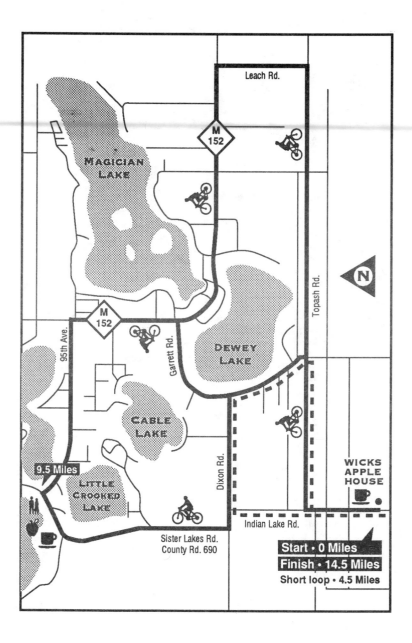

Leach Rd.

M 152

MAGICIAN LAKE

Topash Rd.

N

M 152

95th Ave.

Garrett Rd.

DEWEY LAKE

CABLE LAKE

Dixon Rd.

9.5 Miles

LITTLE CROOKED LAKE

WICKS APPLE HOUSE

Indian Lake Rd.

Sister Lakes Rd.
County Rd. 690

Start • 0 Miles
Finish • 14.5 Miles
Short loop • 4.5 Miles

Faded barns and open farmfields are part of the cycling scenery in southwest Michigan.

After passing through a residential section turn left onto Leach Road at the stop sign at 3.3 miles. Just ahead on your right at 3.4 miles is the historic Sacred Heart of Mary Catholic Church with a cemetery on a hill. In 1838, Chief Leopold Pokagon of the Potawatomi Indians built a log church here on what was then an old Indian graveyard. Eventually he deeded the 40 acres of land to the Catholic bishop of Detroit, and in 1844, Father Theophile Marifault became the church's first permanent priest. Louis Baroux followed, served from 1847-1879, and was buried in the cemetery in 1897. Also buried here in 1841 was Chief Pokagon.

The tour continues from the historic church down a moderate hill at 3.8 miles. You'll cycle past a variety of orchards, including cherries, as well as more cornfields. At 4.4 miles turn left on M-152, a hilly road that can be busy in the summer but is relatively wide with gravel shoulders. You'll enjoy a mixture of residential homes and rolling cornfields before tackling another uphill stretch at 5.5 miles, highlighted by a faded red barn, and then a downhill run curving sharply to your right. The road twists and curves but provides good views of Dewey Lake on the left followed by an uphill segment at 6.1 miles.

At 6.5 miles turn left on Garrett Road as it continues to skirt the shoreline of Dewey Lake. A lot of boating and water skiers will be seen on the water during the summer before you enter the shaded relief of a tunnel of trees at 7 miles.

Turn right on Dixon Road at 7.1 miles, another well shaded stretch of pavement, and continue straight on the road after stopping for the intersection with Indian Lake Road at 7.7 miles. Just beyond, there is a scenic cemetery and then Dixon Road curves to the right and becomes Sister Lakes Road. More apples and cherries orchards are passed as you follow the winding Sister Lakes Road north. This stretch is level and is a leisurely ride past views of Little Crooked Lake and the cottages that line its shore. You enter Van Buren County at 8.9 miles followed by an uphill segment that curves sharply to your right to within view of Round Lake at 9.2 miles. The road curves left and just ahead is the Driftwood Summer Shop, offering T-shirts, souvenirs, beach supplies, and of course, ice cream. Time to take a break, stretch those legs and enjoy a sweet treat! There are more food choices in Sister Lakes; just cycle north on Sister Lake Road to reach the small town and add more distance to this circuit.

Stage two (5 miles) From Driftwood Summer Shop at 9.5 miles, take a right on 95th Avenue where there is a directional arrow. This stretch of 95th Avenue is a narrow road that twists and curves between Little Crooked and Big Crooked lakes, which at one time was a single body of water. These lakes are the highlight of this lakeshore amble as you'll be almost surrounded by water. At 9.7 miles the road curves to the left and climbs a small hill. Turn right at M-152 at 10.5 miles to quickly enter Cass County. After passing a hot dog and ice cream stand (time for another break?) at 11.3 miles, you turn right on Garrett Road and repeat an earlier segment of the road.

With Dewey Lake on your left, you'll cycle past the Shady Shores Resort at 12.3 miles. The resort features cottages, trailer sites and a beach and recreational area. From Shady Shores it's a few more curves past more swaying cornfields to reach Topash Street at 13.2 miles. Backtrack along Topash and turn left on Indian Lake Road at 14.2 miles to reach Wicks' Apple House in less than a third of a mile. Time to browse for gifts at Wicks', purchase cider for the trip home, or sample one of their many tasty desserts!

Shorter option (4.5 miles) From Wicks' Apple House, cycle north on Indian Lake Road and turn right on Topash Street. Follow with a left on Garrett Road and then another left on Dixon Road. Finish the short route by turning left on Indian Lake Road and cycling back to Wicks' Apple House.

Bicycle sales, repair
Bike Specialists, 603 N. 2nd St., Niles; (616) 683-3100.
Baker's Bike Shop Inc., 135 Dixie Way S., South Bend, Indiana; (219) 277-8866.
Wegner's Cyclery, 2621 Niles, St. Joseph; (616) 983-2453.
Area attractions
Wicks' Apple House, Dowagiac; (616) 782-7306.
Tree-Mendus Fruit Farm, Eau Claire; (616) 782-7101.
Area events and festivals
June: Fishing Contest, Sister Lakes.
July: Doe-Waj-Jack Fun Festival, Dowagiac; International Cherry Pit Spitting Championship, Eau Claire; Fourth of July fireworks, Lions Park, Sister Lakes.
September: Flirt with Fall Fest, Sister Lakes.
October: Ciderfest, Wicks' Apple House, Dowagiac.
Travel information
Southwestern Michigan Tourist Council; (616) 925-6301.

4 Blossomland

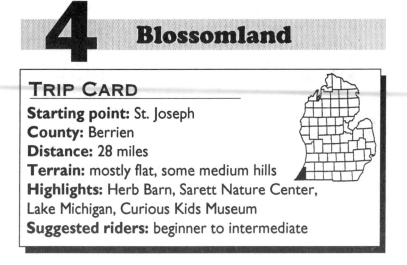

TRIP CARD

Starting point: St. Joseph
County: Berrien
Distance: 28 miles
Terrain: mostly flat, some medium hills
Highlights: Herb Barn, Sarett Nature Center, Lake Michigan, Curious Kids Museum
Suggested riders: beginner to intermediate

From Lake Michigan, across the St. Joseph River, into fruit growing farms in Benton Township and back to the lakeshore again, cyclists will find this 28-mile route that circles the St. Joseph/Benton Harbor area a pleasant journey.

This route will underscore the best of what southwestern Michigan has to offer; beautiful beaches, terrific shopping, lush fruit growing areas, parks and country backroads. Plan to spend the entire day. There's a place to pause and relax at each of the four stages. This route begins near downtown St. Joseph, which has enjoyed a renaissance. Whether you're looking for antiques, gourmet popcorn, educational toys, a kite to fly at the beach or a colorful windsock, you can find it in downtown St. Joseph. Most of the shops are located on State Street, a quaint red brick road. A block west and running parallel to State Street, is Lake Boulevard bordering a park located on a bluff overlooking Lake Michigan, the site of St. Joseph's annual art fair every July.

All-day parking can be found between Lake Boulevard on the bluff and along the 400 block of State Street. You can't miss the parking lot, it's next to the Curious Kids Museum. Be sure to begin or end your ride with a visit to this fun hands-on museum. Next stop; the Herb Barn in Benton Township. Everything for growing, enjoying or sharing herb lore is sold in the "barn", which is surrounded by a greenhouse and many demonstration herb gardens.

The third stage of the trip rambles through orchards, farmlands, and gently rolling hills, where roadside vegetable stands offer the bounty of the season. There are lots of fruits and vegetables grown in the area with something always ripe and ready to eat. Plan a stop at the scenic Sarett Nature Center for an extended rest, a walk in the woods, or to do a little birding. Bikes are not allowed on the Sarett trails, but you can stretch your legs with a stroll to the Paw Paw River.

Another highlight on this route is a heart-pounding, twisting ride down Rocky Gap Road through a canopy of trees, perched high alongside Lake Michigan. Rocky Gap Park, with a scenic overlook is an ideal final stopover before heading back to St. Joseph. Along with enjoying the overlook, you can also walk down the dunes to a sandy Lake Michigan beach to sunbathe in summer or watch the lapping waves on a crisp fall afternoon. If you didn't go "jump in the lake" at Rocky Gap, you can at St. Joseph's Silver Beach. Even if you enjoyed a hearty picnic lunch along the way, you'll be glad to know that downtown St. Joseph has plenty of fine eating establishments. Schu's Grill & Bar, on Lake Boulevard, and Zitta's (known for its burgers) at the train depot, near Silver Beach, offer outdoor dining for the cyclist who just can't bear to be indoors after a ride.

Stage one (6.7 miles) From Lake Boulevard in downtown St. Joseph, go east (right) on Broad Street. You will cross busy Main Street in a quarter mile and then curve right where Broad Street becomes Langley Avenue. Pass Clementine's Restaurant (a nice restaurant on the St. Joseph River) on your left at .6 miles and Kiwanis Park, a city park, a quarter mile down the road before turning left on Napier Avenue at 1.6 miles. In a quarter mile, you'll reach the St. Joseph River where you need to *WALK YOUR BIKE*

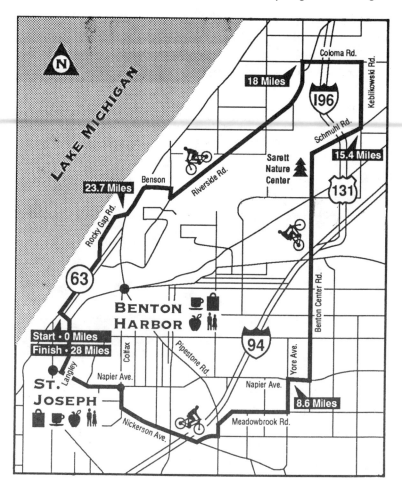

ACROSS THE BRIDGE. Also be alert as the traffic can often be heavy here.

Continue on Napier Avenue to Colfax Avenue; turn right. Turn left on Nickerson Avenue at 3.4 miles and continue biking past M-139, which can be a busy intersection most times. Take the right fork and then turn at the first left after the expressway overpass. Follow this road around the curve onto Townline Road. At 5.6 miles take a left on Pipestone Road and then turn right on

47

Cyclist views the St. Joesph Lighthouse from the city pier.

Meadowbrook Road, where located across the street is the Southwestern Michigan Tourist Council headquarters, a great place for area information (maps, brochures). Also nearby are a Bob Evans restaurant, gas station and an expressway ramp which makes this a busy corner. Be careful!

Just up Meadowbrook Road at 6.5 miles into tour, turn left onto Greenley Road for your first stop; The Herb Barn (616-927-2044). This scenic barn has been converted into an indoor/outdoor shop selling herbs, plants, planters, candles, seasonal decorations, seeds, garden supplies, etc. This is a wonderfully sweet-smelling shopping and a learning experience - worth a lengthy visit.

Stage two (7.1 miles) From the Herb Barn, backtrack a

quarter mile to Meadowbrook Road and turn left (east). At 7.9 miles turn left onto Yore Avenue and head north to Napier Avenue where at 8.6 miles you turn right, just past Lake Michigan College. Go east on Napier Avenue for a half mile and then turn left (north) on Benton Center Road at 9.1 miles. This road passes through a flat stretch of open country where picturesque farms and vineyards make it an exhilarating stretch for the cyclist. You cross Empire Avenue at 9.9 miles and pass through a stand of hardwoods at 12.6 miles. Continue north and at 13.8 miles you'll reach Sarett Nature Center (616-927-4832), your second stop.

Sarett Nature Center is a 400-acre preserve for viewing wildlife in its natural habitat. There's an excellent exhibit area, five miles of walking trails, glassed-in viewing areas and a gift shop for nature lovers. Sarett also has a nice spot for a picnic lunch.

Stage three (4.2 miles) From the nature center, turn left (north) on Benton Center Road which quickly becomes Schmuhl Road. Part of Schmuhl is gravel, so those with 12-speed touring bikes may want to walk their bikes and push them up the hill. The road is still gravel as it descends through a tunnel of trees at 14.4 miles. At 14.7 miles, gravel turns to pavement as Schmuhl curves east and this uphill ride is followed by another long, gradual ascent at 15.1 miles. Just past the expressway overpass, take a left (north) on Kerlikowski Road at 15.4 miles, where you will cycle by some of the orchards that make Southwest Michigan a cornucopia of fruit. Continue north until you reach Coloma Road at 16.9 miles where you turn left (west) at a Marathon gas station. This road can be busy but you depart it within a mile at the next right (south), which is Riverside Road, to enter Riverside. In this small town, on the corner of Fikes and Riverside, you will find a grocery store called Moore's. This red and white building with an outside bench has small-town appeal and is a great place for refreshments and a short break.

Stage four (10 miles) From Moore's, head southwest on

The Herb Barn, one of the attractions along the Blossomland Tour.

Riverside Road. This road angles south and west toward Lake Michigan and along the way you'll cycle over railroad tracks, past the Riverside Post Office and through scenic stretches of open country, orchards and a stand of hardwood trees. Riverside Road ends at Paw Paw Avenue where you take a sharp right on Paw Paw Avenue and then an immediate left on Benson Road at 22.4 miles.

Continue west on Benson Road until it ends at M-63. Turn left on M-63 at 23.1 miles and follow the highway south along another busy stretch of road. Be patient, it doesn't last long. At 23.7 miles you turn right from M-63 onto Rocky Gap Road. While a bit hilly, this road is the highlight of the day for many because of the canopy of trees that shade the road and the scenic views of Lake Michigan. Rocky Gap twists while staying within view of Lake Michigan most of the time. There is a panoramic lookout of Lake Michigan at 24.4 miles.

Turn right at Higman Park Road at 24.9 miles. Follow this road around the curve until it ends at Klock Road and turn right onto the one-way street. Soon Klock becomes Upton Drive and you continue south as the road curves sharply to your left and up a hill to the Blossomland Bridge. Although St. Joseph doesn't have a spectacular skyline; a water tower, historic Whitcomb Hotel and church steeple tells you there's a small, pleasing city just ahead.

At the top of the hill there's a traffic light. Turn right and *WALK YOUR BIKE ACROSS THE BRIDGE.* To reach Silver Beach Park, turn right again at the next traffic light at 26.7 miles and then turn right at a three-way stop sign (Water Street) and descend a steep hill, following the St. Joseph River to its mouth on Lake Michigan. Zitta's Tap & Grill, located in the old St. Joseph train depot, will be on your left. The road curves sharply to your right and ends at Lake Michigan, near Silver Beach, at 27.2 miles. The name of this road changes from Water Street to Vine Street to Broad Street, although it is not as confusing as it sounds. Just look towards Lake Michigan and you won't get lost.

Backtrack the way you came, up the steep hill curving to your right to reach Lake Boulevard. The St. Joseph bandshell, where free

51

concerts are hosted throughout the summer, is on your right at 27.7 miles. Turn left on Lake Boulevard. Schu's (for outdoor dining) is on your left at 27.8 miles and the bluff overlooking Lake Michigan is to your right. You are back to the starting point near the Curious Kids Museum at 28 miles. Time to visit the museum, sit on a bench overlooking Lake Michigan, or dine at a St. Joseph restaurant.

Bicycle sales, service
Wegner's Schwinn Cyclery, 2621 Niles Ave., St. Joseph; (616) 983-2453.

Area attractions
The Herb Barn, Benton Harbor; (616) 927-2044.
Sarett Nature Center, Benton Harbor; (616) 927-4832.
Curious Kids Museum, St. Joseph; (616) 983-2543.

Area events and festivals
May: Blossomtime Festival, Benton Harbor, St. Joseph.
July: St. Joseph Art Fair; Venetian Festival, St. Joseph.
September: Tri-State Regatta Festival, St. Joseph.

Travel information
Southwestern Michigan Tourist Council, (616) 925-6301.
St. Joseph Today, (616) 982-6739.
Lake Michigan Convention & Visitors Bureau, (616) 925-6100.

5 Amish Tour

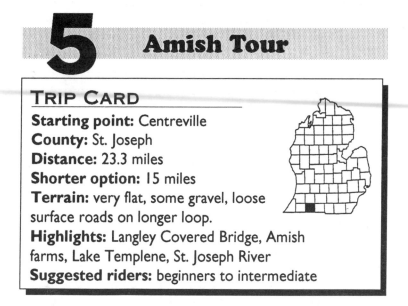

TRIP CARD

Starting point: Centreville
County: St. Joseph
Distance: 23.3 miles
Shorter option: 15 miles
Terrain: very flat, some gravel, loose surface roads on longer loop.
Highlights: Langley Covered Bridge, Amish farms, Lake Templene, St. Joseph River
Suggested riders: beginners to intermediate

Built in 1887, with three spans of 94 feet, the Langley Covered Bridge is the longest of Michigan's few remaining covered bridges. This one-lane bridge, located north of Centreville in St. Joseph County, was built of the highest quality white pine. Over the years, this landmark has been preserved and stands as a living reminder of a bygone era.

Cyclists are naturally drawn to covered bridges, probably because there are so few of these nostalgic structures left in Michigan. The Langley Covered Bridge is definitely the highlight of this 23-mile bicycle route that begins in Centreville. It is best to ride this route on a mountain or hybrid bicycle because some of the roads are gravel or loose textured.

The 23-mile route and the 15-mile shorter option are mostly flat. Traveling unpaved roads, cyclists will be inspired by the simplicity of the Amish people who live in this country setting. On Sunday afternoons, many Amish family members can be seen in buggies with horses trotting along at a slower speed than the slowest cyclist in your group! No electrical lines lead into their simple farm homes. The bright orange safety reflectors on the back of their buggies stand out in contrast to their dark, 19th century-style clothing. This ride will soothe the nerves of city dwellers as it winds through wooded areas, cornfields (after all, St. Joseph County is just north of LaGrange County, Indiana, a state where corn is king), man-made Lake Templene, residential homes and the placid St. Joseph River.

Your cares will evaporate into the country air when you realize that the only decision to be made in an afternoon of cycling here is whether to eat at the Covered Bridge Inn in Centreville, grab a sandwich and candy bar at the Village Market, or tackle a pizza or sandwich at Angelo's Pizza & Subs at the starting point in Centreville. On the shorter loop, you might have to decide on a flavor of Hudsonville ice cream at the Sand Lake Ice Cream and Party Store in the small town of Nottawa.

St. Joseph County is sometimes overlooked when people search for a perfect weekend getaway or a fun, one-day outing. The small towns, waterways, bed & breakfast establishments, entertaining festivals and canoeing and biking opportunities make this accessible county a unique destination; one of those quiet surprises! The two routes in this chapter were adapted from a booklet published by the River Country Tourism Council and created by Diane Ruggles, manager of the Bicycle Rack, a popular bike shop in Three Rivers. Her comprehensive booklet describes 12 interconnecting routes in St. Joseph County, complete with maps and detailed information (for address see page 58).

Today, the sleepy town of Colon, in the eastern part of the county, is home to the Abbott's Magic Manufacturing Company (616-432-3235) which builds 2,000 magic tricks and gadgets. Every August, amateur and professional magicians congregate in the village for a series of shows at the high school auditorium. Magical memorabilia can be seen at the Colon Community Museum.

Stage one (3.9 miles) Beginning at Village Market parking

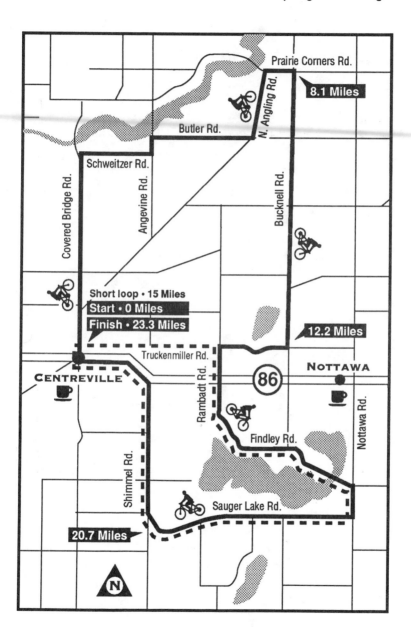

Prairie Corners Rd.

8.1 Miles

N. Angling Rd.

Butler Rd.

Schweitzer Rd.

Angevine Rd.

Covered Bridge Rd.

Bucknell Rd.

Short loop • 15 Miles

Start • 0 Miles

Finish • 23.3 Miles

12.2 Miles

Truckenmiller Rd.

CENTREVILLE

Rambadt Rd.

86

NOTTAWA

Nottawa Rd.

Findley Rd.

Shimmel Rd.

Sauger Lake Rd.

20.7 Miles

N

Langley Covered Bridge, north of Centreville in St. Joseph County, is the longest one in Michigan.

lot in Centreville, turn left on M-86. The Covered Bridge Inn appears on your right at 0.8 miles and immediately after passing it turn right (north) onto Covered Bridge Road. You will soon be cycling through a mix of woodlands and open country. This is also Amish country and cyclists need to respect their horses and buggies on the road as they often move along at a slower pace. Never accidentally spook a horse. Let them know what you are going to do or that you are approaching them. If they see you early they will rarely bolt. Remember, gently speak to the horse, but never touch them without asking permission from the owner first.

Covered Bridge Road is a paved, flat road with no shoulders that at 3.9 miles crosses the St. Joseph River on the Langley

Covered Bridge. At 282 feet, the structure is the longest covered bridge in Michigan and one of the heaviest at 3 tons. Built in 1887, the Langley Bridge had to be raised 8 feet to avoid the surging waters when the Sturgis Dam was completed in 1910.

Nearby is Covered Bridge Park, a 15-acre park that features tables, grills and a good view of the historic bridge. Take a short break at this scenic spot if for no other reason than to rearrange your gear for the rest of the tour.

Stage two (10.3 miles) Just south of the covered bridge, turn right (east) on Schweitzer Road. This is an unpaved road of packed dirt that passes through a mixture of hardwood trees and cultivated fields - a great road for a mountain bicycle! The pavement returns when you turn left (north) on Angevine Road and then immediately turn right (east) on Butler Road at 5.2 miles. This road is paved at first and then becomes a stretch of gravel through more hardwoods and abundant farmfields. At 6.6 miles turn left (north) on North Angling, another gravel road that leads to more scattered forested areas in a third of a mile, and then turn right on paved Prairie Corners Road at 7.7 miles.

Turn right (south) on Bucknell Road at 8.1 miles, a gravel road that heads south past Amish farms with horses and windmills, but not a single power line. A rather amazing sight in our day and age. Eventually you cycle over a one-lane bridge and a few rolling hills before turning right (west) on Truckenmiller Road at 12.2 miles, another gravel road. This road curves sharply to your left at 12.7 miles past Evans Lake, and then sharply to your right. Finish the second stage by turning left on Rambadt Road at 13.3 miles.

Stage three (10 miles) Keep cycling south on Rambadt Road across M-86 at 13.9 miles. This portion of the road is paved and when it curves to your left, it becomes Findley Road. Findley curves around Lake Templene at 14.3 miles, a man-made lake that was created when small streams in the area were dammed. At 14.5 miles there are good views of Lake Templene to your right just before the road curves sharply south through a pleasant residential area and small farms near the lake. The road continues to wind past the lake, agricultural fields and at one point a picturesque, faded white barn, with noisy roosters in the barnyard. At 17.1 miles turn right (south) on Nottawa Road and then right (west) on Sauger Lake Road at 17.5 miles. This is a paved road with a pleasant mix of trees, residential homes and more views of Lake Templene. Wildflowers often grow between the water and the road throughout much of the summer.

Beginning at 19.4 miles the road twists and curves and within a half mile you cycle by Glen Oaks Community College. (to lengthen this route, you can cycle through the campus and enjoy the view from the hill overlooking Lake Templene). At 20.7 miles turn right (north) on Shimmel Road, a paved avenue with gravel shoulders and more traffic than the rest of the route. Finish your day by turning left (west) on busy M-86 at 22 miles. You are now back in the village of Centreville and will reach at 23.3 miles the Village Market parking lot.

Shorter option (15 miles) This entire route is on paved roads, making it ideal for 10 or 12-speed tour bicycles. Turn left out of the Village Market parking lot in Centreville onto M-86. Cycle three blocks to Clinton Road; turn right. Cycle one block to Market Street; turn right (east) and this road soon becomes Truckenmiller Road. Turn right (south) on Rambadt Road, a road that winds down by Lake Templene and becomes Findley Road. Turn right (south) on Nottawa Road (or turn left on Nottawa Road and cycle into the town of Nottawa for an ice cream break at the Sand Lake Party Store & Ice Cream). Turn right (west) on Sauger Lake Road (also County Road 147) and then right (north) on Shimmel Road (also County Road 138) to return to M-86 where you head left for the Village Market parking lot.

Bicycle service, sales
The Kickstand, Maple Lane Plaza, 1100 North Main St., Three

Rivers; (616) 278-7305.

Cottin's Hardware, Sturgis Plaza, Sturgis; (616) 651-9286.

The Kickstand Schwinn Cyclery, 1303 East Chicago Rd., Sturgis; (616) 651-5088.

Village Cyclery, 148 N. Grand, Schoolcraft; (616) 679-4242.

Area attractions

Abbott's Magic Manufacturing Co., Colon; (616) 432-3235. Colon Community Museum, Colon.

Area events and festivals

June: Three Rivers Water Festival, Three Rivers.

July: Covered Bridge Days, Centreville.

August: Colon Magic Festival, Colon.

September: St. Joseph County Grange Fair, Centreville; Fall Tour bikeathon, Sturgis.

October: Three Rivers Color Tour, Three Rivers.

Travel information

River Country Tourism Council, Box 70, Centreville, MI 49032; (616) 467-4505 or 1-800-447-282 (free 20-page booklet available on 12 bicycle routes in St. Joseph County. Detailed information).

St. Joseph County Parks & Recreation; (616) 467-6361.

Sturgis Chamber of Commerce; (616) 651-5758

Three Rivers Area Chamber of Commerce; (616) 278-8193.

A cyclist pauses on one of the many rail-trails that been developed in Michigan from abandoned railroads.

6 Kal-Haven Trail

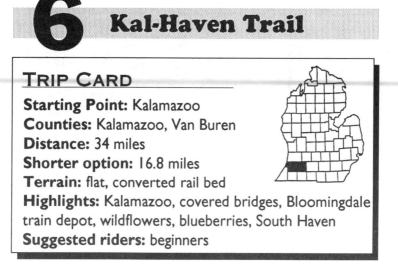

TRIP CARD

Starting Point: Kalamazoo
Counties: Kalamazoo, Van Buren
Distance: 34 miles
Shorter option: 16.8 miles
Terrain: flat, converted rail bed
Highlights: Kalamazoo, covered bridges, Bloomingdale train depot, wildflowers, blueberries, South Haven
Suggested riders: beginners

Imagine a trail from one of Michigan's largest cities to one of its nicest resort towns. Imagine a relaxing journey past blueberry fields, wildflowers, through quaint villages...a tour that takes you over seven bridges. Imagine no more, it's the Kal-Haven Trail, a route where friendly folks greet you along the way, ask you how far you've come, and give suggestions on where to eat.

This woodsy trail makes you feel like a kid again on a grand adventure! At one point, west of Gobles, my friend and I were pleasantly refreshed by the peaceful aura of the route. At this exceptionally scenic spot along the 34-mile journey, you will find a babbling brook with wildflowers interspersed between rocks and water. This cycling adventure into the woods and country is easily accessible for many city dwellers, whether they live in Chicago, Kalamazoo, South Bend or Grand Rapids.

The Kal-Haven Trail Sesquicentennial State Park is an abandoned rail line linking Kalamazoo to South Haven. The route attracted railroad builders as early as 1836, a year before Michigan

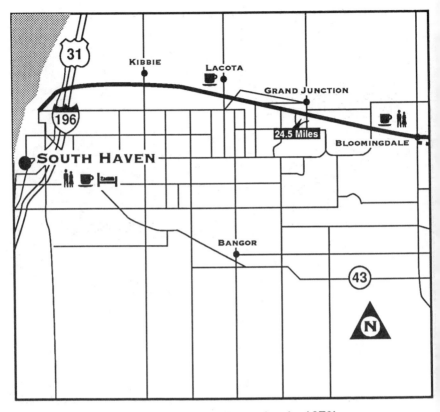

statehood, and when the railroads prospered in the 1870's, towns popped up. Today, these same towns now provide food and lodging for cyclists and other trail users who have replaced rail passengers. As the rail was routed to avoid steep hills, this 34-mile trail is flat - ideal for beginning mountain bicyclists.

Much of the trail is made of crushed screened cinder slag or crushed screened limestone, which is best for mountain or hybrid bicycles, although 10 or 12-speed road bicycles are acceptable. I usually ride a 12-speed bicycle but used my mountain bike on the Kal-Haven Trail. Mountain bicycles allow you to lean more freely from side to side or sit upright for a better view of the natural surroundings. The Kal-Haven is best cycled at a leisurely pace so

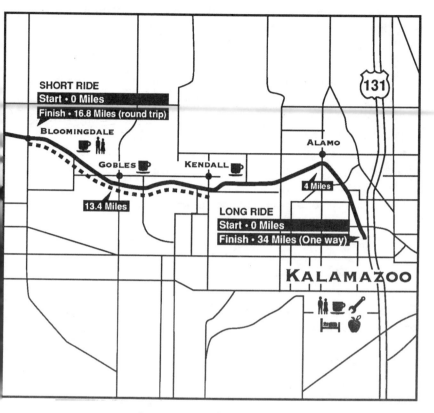

you can stop often to enjoy the scenery.

Trail Fees: This rails-to-trails approach to park management is similar to the Hart-Montague Trail in Oceana County; the trail was built as a state park and is now jointly operated by the Friends of the Kal-Haven Trail and the Michigan Department of Natural Resources. The Friends of the Kal-Haven Trail finance the operation and maintenance of the trail through user fees, fundraisers and private donations.

Annual or day passes are required and can be purchased at the east and west trailheads, the Van Buren State Park, at the depot caboose in Bloomingdale, from trail rangers or at any business displaying the trail logo. In South Haven, trail passes can be purchased at several locations, including Cousin's Restaurant and Campground on Blue Star Highway, Dale's True Value Hardware on Blue Star Highway and the South Haven Chamber of Commerce on Quaker Street.

The romance of the railroad era comes alive in the town of Bloomingdale with its historic, refurbished train depot, and a caboose that serves as an information center. It is a great spot to begin or end your ride, if you don't want to pedal the whole trail. Bloomingdale has parking for vehicles as well as restaurants and shops. Approximately 8 miles from Kalamazoo is Mentha, where nearby fields of flat, dark and very moist soil were once the world's largest producer of peppermint and spearmint.

Then there is Kalamazoo, a pleasant city of 80,000 and home of Western Michigan University. Kalamazoo has a variety of attractions and activities to enjoy before or after your ride or for non-cyclists who agree to wait for you. There is an aviation history museum in Kalamazoo, a classic car museum in nearby Hickory Corners and the Celery Flats Interpretive Center, in Portage, that traces the history when the area was renown for its celery farms.

Stage one (9.9 miles) The east trailhead is near Kalamazoo, just west of US-131 and 2 miles north of M-43, on 10th Street in Oshtemo Township (follow the signs). The staging area includes parking for 150 vehicles, trail signs, a picnic area, toilets and a renovated caboose that serves as an information center and is manned by volunteers during the summer.

In the beginning, the trail winds northward and across the first of seven bridges that were previously railroad trestles. The initial stretch is through a hilly area that is especially pretty in the spring when wildflowers are in full bloom. It's hard not to be impressed with the woods and natural surrounding of this leg of the route.

The next bridge is near Mentha, where the land changes to flat, open fields, and is followed by another bridge (an old cattle crossing) as you approach Kendall, located just north of the trail, 9.9 miles from the eastern trailhead. A unique stop near Kendall is

The depot and caboose/information center at Bloomingdale.

the Bee Hive Farm, a tourist trap if there ever was one. But it does have a bakery where you can obtain refreshments. In Kendall, you'll also find restrooms and better places for refreshments.

Stage two (8.4 miles) Continue west from Kendall and in 3.5 miles, you arrive at Gobles, another small, unpretentious town. In Gobles, try an old-fashioned soda or malt at Spaydes Gobles Pharmacy or have a sandwich at the deli at the Gobles Grocery. The hardware store at the intersection of M-40 and the trail rents bicycles, including tandems. The next town west of Gobles is Bloomingdale, reached at 18.3 miles from the eastern trailhead. Bloomingdale, with its wonderfully restored depot, is a popular place to park your car to pedal only a portion of the trail as opposed to the entire 34 miles. For food, Bloomingdale has the 4-Way Stop Grocery with a deli, located just 300 feet east of the trail information center. Something more filling? There also is the Bloomingdale Cafe, famous for its spicy wet burritos.

Stage three (15.8 miles) From Bloomingdale, get back in the saddle, and - you guessed it - head west. You'll cycle over an intriguing old camelback bridge crossing Barber Creek and then past the towns of Grand Junction at 24.5 miles and Lacota at 27.4 miles. In both villages, there are several choices for food (do we ever stop eating? No!), including hand-dipped ice cream at the Lacota Quick Stop and fresh sandwiches at the Country Cupboard in Grand Junction.

From Lacota, there is less than 7 miles to the trail's end. Keep heading west. The largest trestle, now a scenic covered bridge, spans the Black River, near South Haven. At 34.1 miles you've reached your final destination; the resort community of South Haven, located on Lake Michigan. The South Haven trailhead is temporary as plans call for it to be moved closer to the downtown area in 1994. It's presently located on Blue Star Highway, 0.75 mile south of North Shore Road where you'll find a small, gravel parking lot and vault toilets. There is no water here.

South Haven is home to the Michigan Maritime Museum, art galleries, gift shops, bed & breakfast establishments and, of course, inviting Lake Michigan beaches. Just south of town is the Van Buren State Park, a great place to set up camp or to enjoy a picnic.

Shorter option (16.8 miles) From the train depot in Bloomingdale, head east on the trail, by the town of Gobles, and then by Kendall. Stop in Gobles or Kendall along the way, and then backtrack to Bloomingdale.

Bicycle sales, service

Alfred E. Bike, 320 E. Michigan Ave., Kalamazoo; (616) 349-9423.

Billy's Bike Shop, 80 E. Michigan, Galesburg; (616) 665-5202.

Breakaway Bicycles, 5742 S. Westnedge Ave., Kalamazoo; (616) 349-5555.

Millwood Schwinn, 1015 E. Cork Rd., Kalamazoo; (616) 349-6384.

Parchment Bicycle, 5348 Riverview, Parchment; (616) 343-8118.

Portage Schwinn Cyclery, 300 E. Centre, Portage; (616) 327-3393.

Riverview Equipment & Bait, 53804 County Road-687, Hartford; (616) 621-4791.

Safety Cycle Ski & Sport, 1908 W. Main St., Kalamazoo; (616) 381-7233.

Vern's Sport & Cycle, 189 10th St., Plainwell; (616) 685-6626.

Vornkamp Bike, 673 Lake, Kalamazoo; (616) 344-3599.

Area events and festivals

April: Kitefest, Kalamazoo.

May: Kal-Haven Trail Blazer; Mayfair, Kalamazoo.

June: Celery Flats Arts & Craft Fair, Portage.

July: National Blueberry Festival, South Haven; Flowerfest, Kalamazoo.

September: Celery Fest, Portage; Michigan Wine & Harvest Festival, Paw Paw.

Area attractions

Gilmore Car Museum, Hickory Corners; (616) 671-5089.

Kalamazoo Aviation Museum, Kalamazoo; (616) 382-6555.

Celery Flats Interpretive Center, Portage; (616) 329-4522.

Kalamazoo Public Museum; (616) 345-7092.

Kalamazoo Nature Center; (616)381-1574.

Wine Country Scenic Train, Paw Paw; (616) 657-5963.

St. Julian Winery, Paw Paw; (616) 657-5568

Warner Vineyards, Paw Paw; (616) 657-3165.

Michigan Maritime Museum, South Haven; (616) 637-8078.

Travel information

Kal-Haven Trail; (616) 637-2788, (616) 637-4984.

Kalamazoo Convention & Visitors Bureau; (616) 381-4003.

Paw Paw Chamber of Commerce; (616) 657-5395.

Lakeshore Convention & Visitors Bureau, South Haven; (616) 637-5252.

South Haven Chamber of Commerce; (616) 637-5171.

The Saugatuck Chain Ferry crosses the Kalamazoo River.

7 Saugatuck Tour

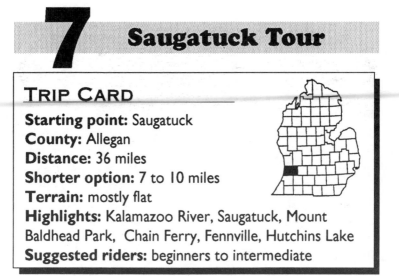

TRIP CARD

Starting point: Saugatuck
County: Allegan
Distance: 36 miles
Shorter option: 7 to 10 miles
Terrain: mostly flat
Highlights: Kalamazoo River, Saugatuck, Mount Baldhead Park, Chain Ferry, Fennville, Hutchins Lake
Suggested riders: beginners to intermediate

Tucked away off of I-196 on the Kalamazoo River, near Lake Michigan is the town of Saugatuck. Trendy boutiques, art galleries and restaurants accessible by boat as well as cars are all a part of busy Saugatuck. Maybe it's the ambience, but visitors to this resort town always seem relaxed and happy. As the bed & breakfast capital of Michigan, Saugatuck boasts more than 15 of these establishments, from Victorian homes to country settings. Moored at the edge of its downtown shopping district is an impressive armada of cabin cruisers, yachts and bobbing sailboats.

The shorter loop of this circuit, 7.2-10.4 miles, has to be one of the most scenic in West Michigan and, in this honeymooner's haunt of a town, can even be called romantic. The route starts in Saugatuck, leads you through shaded woods and spectacular Lake Michigan scenery, and ends with a wonderful opportunity to travel across the Kalamazoo River on a chain-powered ferry.

The start of both loops is at Wicks Park on Water Street, where public restrooms feature an impressionist painting on the side (only in Saugatuck!). This is a great place to lock up your bicycles, after your ride, to go people watching, boat watching (it's debatable which is more intriguing in Saugatuck) or enjoy the town's wide variety of restaurants. Stroll along Butler or Water streets, buy some fudge or that "gotta have it" Saugatuck T-shirt.

The longer 36.7-mile loop winds its way out of Saugatuck to just south of the Holland area then through open countryside to Fennville. Although Fennville is only five miles away from Saugatuck, the two towns are in direct contrast to each other. Sleepy little Fennville is best known for its October Goose Festival. The nearby Allegan State Game area and the Todd Farm attract flocks of Canada geese in the fall and thus goose watchers. During the two-day festival there's a goose calling championship, goose arts and crafts show, a 10-kilometer Wild Goose Chase, and a parade. Or any time of the year you can stop at the Blue Goose Cafe (616-561-5044) for its roasted chicken, a Friday night fish fry or a Blue Goose omelette. The Blue Goose Cafe is an ideal stop halfway through the longer route for a light meal or snack.

Whether you undertake the long or short option, the addition of boat cruises, a chain ferry, dune rides, and a steamship tour with pleasant cycling, food and shopping, add up to a day or two, or even three days, of fun in Allegan County.

Shorter option (7.2 - 10.4 miles) Begin at Wicks Park, on Water Street near the public restrooms and turn right on Lucy Street at 0.1 mile and then immediately right on Butler Street. Walk bicycles in this main shopping area to avoid a collision (and to see what stores you want to stop at later!). Take a left on Culver Street at 0.6 miles, which turns into Lake Street, pedal uphill and then turn right onto Blue Star Highway at 1.3 miles to cross the Kalamazoo River. To the west is Harbor Village where you'll find SS Keewatin Ship Tours, City of Douglas Dinner Cruises and a store to stock up on food and drink.

Turn right (west) on Center Street at 2 miles and head west past two bed and breakfast establishments within a mile. Kirby House, built in 1890, appears first and is followed by the Sherwood

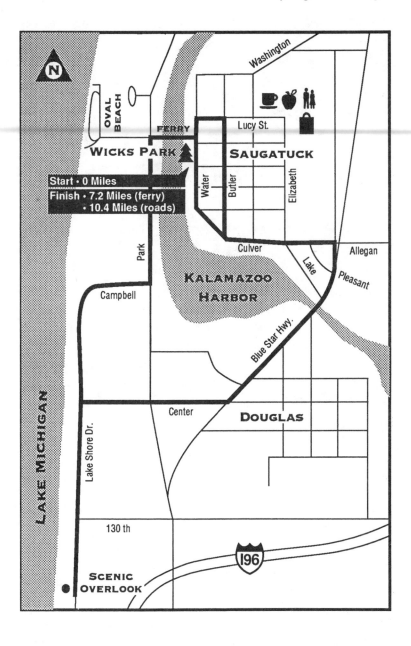

The view of Saugatuck from the top of Mount Baldhead.

Forest Bed and Breakfast, both on the right side of Center Street. At 3 miles, turn left on Lake Shore Drive. This road is narrow but shady as it skirts the edge of a bluff overlooking Lake Michigan. Head south to the Lake Shore Resort (616-857-7121), where there is a great vantage point to enjoy the Lake Michigan shoreline and dunes in the distance.

From the lookout point at Lake Shore Resort, backtrack on Lake Shore Drive. Rosemont Inn, an elegant bed and breakfast, is reached at 5.5 miles and a half mile beyond it you turn right on Shorewood Drive, which turns into Campbell Road. Turn left on Park Street at 6.4 miles and you're back in the Saugatuck city limits.

At 7.2 miles you've arrived at Mount Baldhead Park, where there are restrooms, a shelter and picnic tables. There is also a stairway that leads to the top of the 200-foot dune where you'll find observation decks and a fantastic view of Saugatuck, the Kalamazoo River and Lake Michigan. Trails on the other side lead down to Oval Beach, where MTV once filmed a segment.

Back at the park you have the option of taking the Saugatuck Chain Ferry across the river back to the starting point. It's only $1 for a ride on the only hand-powered ferry in the state. Or you can save a buck by pedaling around the river back to the starting point, via Park Street and then left on Center Street at 8.5 miles. Turn left on Blue Star Highway (caution: can be busy!) at 8.8 miles and finally left on Lake Street at 9.5 miles, which curves to the right into Water Street within a half mile. At 10.4 miles, you're back at Wicks Park.

SAUGATUCK-FENNVILLE LOOP

Stage one (14.7 miles) Head north on Water Street and then turn right on Lucy Street, left on Holland, and then another left on Blue Star Highway at 1.4 miles. Travel for a mile on Blue Star Highway, which can be busy, and just before the I-196 overpass, turn left on 64th Street, where Saugatuck State Park is signposted. Heading north you actually pass within a mile of the entrance to the state park. The undeveloped unit features hiking trails, scenic dunes and uncrowded beaches because it's a mile walk from the parking lot to Lake Michigan.

At 7.6 miles, turn right on 146th Street and head east through the tiny village of Graafschap reached at 9.3 miles. Turn right (south) on 60th Street and within a third of a mile you will be at Nob Hill Country Store. From here you enter rolling open country and tackle an uphill segment at 10.8 miles. At 14.7 miles turn left (east) on 136th Avenue to complete the first stage.

Stage two (7.8 miles) Cycle less than a mile on 136th Avenue to 58th Street and turn right. There's a picturesque Christmas tree farm on your right at 18 miles and horse stables on your left at 21.3 miles. From the stables you'll soon see the "Welcome to Fennville" sign and then turn left (east) onto 124th Street (also labeled M-89), the main road into downtown Fennville. Time for a break, a stroll through the small town or possibly lunch at the Blue Goose Cafe reached at 22.5 miles into the tour. Breakfast is served anytime, so you can load up on carbohydrates

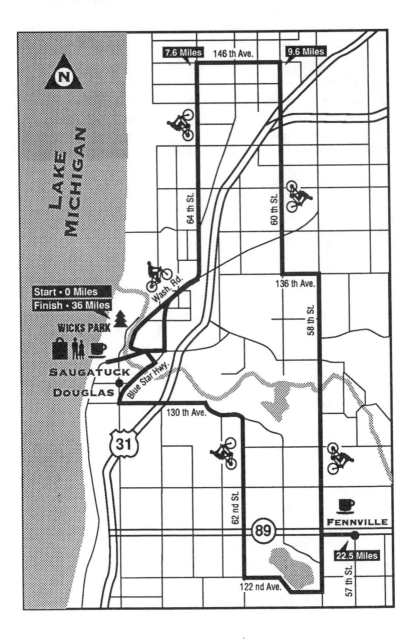

with the cafe's Belgian waffle.

Stage three (13.4 miles) Head west out of Fennville on 124th Street (M-89) back to 58th Avenue and turn left (south) this time. Within two miles this road curves west around Hutchins Lake and becomes 122nd Avenue as you skirt the shoreline. Turn right (north) onto 62nd Street which will lead you past Fenn Valley Vineyards (616-561-2396). At the winery visitors can enjoy a self-guided tour of vineyard and cellar operations, watch an audiovisual program on "wine appreciation" and do a little wine tasting. Just remember you still have another 10 miles left of the tour. Don't get too mellow.

Continue north on 62nd Street, cross 124th Street to Riverside Drive, which veers to the left at 30.6 miles. Although there is little shoulder along Riverside, this is still a pleasant road for cycling as it curves and winds its way back to Douglas. Eventually Riverside turns into 130th Avenue and you're back in Douglas at 32.5 miles. Turn right (north) on Blue Star Highway (caution: busy) at 33.7 miles and then left on Lake Street at 35 miles. From here it's back to Wickes Park and the starting point. Food time (of course!) or simply rest and enjoy the colorful, casual atmosphere of this placid resort community.

Bicycle sales, service

Cross Country Cycle, 137 N. River Ave., Holland; (616) 396-7491.

Highwheeler Bicycle Shop, 211 S. River Ave., Holland; (616) 396-6084.

Holland Schwinn Cyclery, 250 S. River Ave.; Holland; (616) 393-0046.

Area Attractions

"M/V City of Douglas" (scenic, dinner and luncheon cruises); (616) 857-2151, ext. 26, or (616) 857-2107.

Saugatuck Boat Cruises; (616) 857-4261.

Saugatuck Chain Ferry; (616) 857-2151, ext. 26, or (616)857-2107

"SS Keewatin" (Maritime Museum on Great Lakes steamship); (616) 857-2151, ext. 26, or (616) 857-2107.

Fenn Valley Vineyards and Wine Cellar, Fennville; (616) 561-2396

Area events and festivals

July: Harbor Days/Venetian Festival, Saugatuck.

August: Arts and crafts shows, Saugatuck.

September: Jazz Festival, Saugatuck/Douglas.

October: Halloween Harvest Festival, Saugatuck; Goose Festival, Fennville.

Travel information

Saugatuck/Douglas Convention and Visitors Bureau; (616) 857-5801.

Fennville Area Chamber of Commerce; (616) 561-5013 or (616)561-6311.

Holland Area Chamber of Commerce; (616) 392-2389.

Holland Convention & Visitors Bureau; (616) 396-4221.

8 Dutch Delight

TRIP CARD

Starting point: Holland
County: Ottawa
Distance: 51 miles
Shorter option: 20 miles
Terrain: relatively flat, some rolling hills
Highlights: Tunnel Park, Lake Michigan, Dutch attractions, Grand Haven, Holland State Park
Suggested riders: beginners for shorter option, intermediate for longer loop

Riding three abreast on bike trails that follow Lake Michigan and weave in and around a pleasant community- that's the joy of a 51-mile (and 20-mile shorter option) bicycle loop from Holland to Grand Haven. Holland's widespread reputation of a tourist town full of tulips and Dutch attractions has made this area bicycle-friendly for all ages; from a child following Lake Michigan for a mile or so to competitive cyclists looking for a 51-mile training loop.

There are many miles of bike paths in Ottawa County that are separate from roads, yet follow them. One of the highlights of this route is the bike path on Lake Shore Avenue which traverses rolling hills through canopies of trees in full, lush foliage while skirting Lake Michigan. Experienced cyclists can ride this path from Tunnel Park, near Holland State Park, all the way to another delightful tourist town; Grand Haven.

Families whose members have different cycling abilities will also enjoy the area. In the summer, spouse and kids can travel as far as they want to and then backtrack to Holland State Park on

Lake Michigan. While waiting for the more experienced cyclist to finish the longer loop, they can enjoy one of the finest beaches in the state as well as "Big Red", Holland's landmark lighthouse, and numerous eateries nearby.

The longer, 51-mile loop travels for 3.1 miles on James Street, a road that gives you an idea of the Dutch heritage of this town, which offers a wide variety in post-ride options. On the corner of US-31 and James Street is Manufacturers Marketplace with more than 55 brand name outlet stores. It's a true shopper's delight whether you're looking for dish towels to match your Pfaltzgraff dinnerware, sweatpants for the whole family or rock bottom prices on toys.

Near the mall there's also the Country Inn by Carlson (616-396-6677) with its Dutch facade for convenient lodging. At Dutch Village, on the same corner, you can watch wooden shoes being made or shop for handcrafted items. What about food? If you're looking for more than hot dogs-on-the-beach, there's several fine dining establishments in Holland such as the Hatch, 1870 Ottawa Beach Rd., or the Sandpiper, 2225 S. Shore Drive. Better than fast food, but just as cheap, are the three Russ' Restaurants in Holland (616-396-2348), serving West Michigan style meals - lots of food for a moderate price. My friends stumbled upon Spad's Pizza, 2065 Lake St., which sells pizza by the slice, a filling and quick energy booster for cyclists. Near the Holland State Park, there's the Ottawa Beach Inn Restaurant, 2155 Ottawa Beach Rd., perfect for tired, happy cyclists.

Stage one (10.9 miles) From Tunnel Park on Lake Shore Avenue in Holland, head north on the bike path. You'll have to cross a couple of roads and travel partially on the shoulder where it's necessary to watch out for private driveways. But for the most part it's clear sailing to your first stop, Kirk Park, south of Grand Haven. Early in this circuit, you'll find many segments shaded by a canopy of trees, including a half-mile stretch from 1.5 miles to 2 miles. Unlike the mostly flat rail trails, this bike path features a

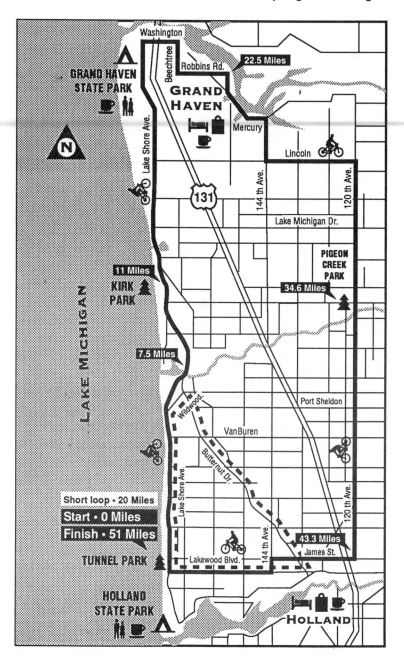

number of rolling but fun hills that also attract walkers, joggers, in-line skaters and other non-motorized users.

At 4.8 miles you pedal through a series of forested rolling hills where in the spring a variety of wildflowers can be spotted along the edge. A bridge spanning the Pigeon River is crossed at 7.5 miles followed by a stretch through open country where the trail is occasionally the shoulder of the road. At 8.6 miles you're back on the bike paths and the last mile before your first stop, Kirk Park, is another delightful ride through a hardwood forest. Ottawa County's Kirk Park is reached at 10.7 miles into the tour and is a good place for an extended break to cool off your feet with a wade in the "big lake." There are also restrooms located in the park.

Stage two (8.4 miles) From Kirk Park, head north on the bike path through another stand of pine before Hiawatha Drive and then across a wooden plank section of the trail at 12.1 miles. The bike path continues along Lake Shore Avenue and is often hidden from the road, as it diverts into the forest offering a pleasant route. There's a cemetery on the right at 14.8 miles, followed by several residential neighborhoods and finally at 18.1 miles you pass the "Welcome to Grand Haven" sign.

In Grand Haven, home of the Musical Fountain, another classic lighthouse and one of the most colorful river walks in the state, you'll travel on sidewalks to Washington Street, the heart of the city, reached at 19.3 miles. Time to stop at a restaurant, take a water break or a side jaunt to Grand Haven State Park that can be reached by following the boardwalk along the Grand River. You'll also find a Russ' Restaurant in Grand Haven at 1313 S. Beacon Blvd.

Stage three (11.7 miles) Turn right on Washington Street in Grand Haven. You'll be traveling on wide sidewalks and immediately will come to a busy corner with Andre's Eatery on the left. Be careful at the busy corners of Beacon Boulevard and turn right (south) on Beechtree at 20.8 miles where you'll pass through an industrial section before taking a left on Robbins Road at 21.5

Holland Harbor Lighthouse across from Holland State Park.

miles.

At this point there are sidewalks on both sides of the road and at 22.2 miles you're back on the bike trails (eeeha!). Pass 160th Avenue and turn right (south) onto Mercury Drive at 22.8 miles to begin a long, level stretch of bike path that's interrupted briefly by a short segment of gravel shoulder. A bayou off the Grand River is crossed at 24.9 miles and nearby on the left is the Bayou Antique Shop. Turn right (south) onto 144th Avenue and then left (east) onto Lincoln Avenue. Refreshment break! At the corner of Lincoln and 128th Avenue is Spinner's Grocery Store for a good dose of junk food. There are no bike paths on Lincoln Street, but the road has fairly light traffic and is a level route through pleasant farm country.

Stage four (12.8 miles) Turn right at the corner of Lincoln Avenue and 120th Avenue and head south on 120th Avenue for more than 10 miles. This stretch is a flat and straight ride through more farmland and Christmas tree farms. This road is an excellent choice when the weather is cooler, allowing you to avoid the sometimes chilly lake breezes. On 120th Avenue you'll pass the Pigeon Creek County Park at 34.6 miles, the South Olive Christian Reformed Church on at 38.4 miles and another brick church on your right at 40.2 miles. As can clearly be seen from this road, the Holland area is a stronghold for the Christian Reformed Church which was formed here in 1857. It's been estimated that a third of the denomination's members live in West Michigan.

At 43.3 miles is the intersection of James Street and 120th Avenue, the end of the fourth stage. Time to get off the bike, stretch your legs and prepare for the short and final leg back to Tunnel Park.

Stage five (7.6 miles) Turn right (west) on James Street and soon you'll be back on the bike trails. Travel to corner of James Street and US-31 where you'll find a Wendy's Old Fashioned Hamburgers on your left along with Manufacturer's Marketplace, Westshore Mall and Dutch Village - all pre and post ride options. You've rode 43.8 miles when you reach this bustling shopping area. Use caution to cross the busy highway and continue heading west on James Street and cross Butternut Drive. Turn left on Division (144th Avenue) where you'll still be on the narrow bike trail.

At 46.9 miles, turn right on Lakewood Boulevard. Go up a slight hill, cross 152nd Avenue and at 48.9 miles, pass another Christian Reformed church, a stately red brick structure on your right. More rolllling, rolllllling hills; a fun stretch for everybody! And then it's back to Lake Shore Avenue where you turn left to get back to the starting point at Tunnel Park. Or else stay on the trail for 1.6 miles to reach Lake Macatawa. From here you can turn right (west) on 168th to continue to Holland State Park for a stroll on the beach or to take in the catamarans, sailboats and other boats entering Lake Michigan. Food??? The Ottawa Beach Inn Restaurant is

The riverwalk and lighthouse in Grand Haven.

located near the entrance of the state park.

Shorter option (20 miles) Head north out of Tunnel Park on the bike paths and pass Quincy, Ransom, New Holland and Van Buren streets. Turn right on Wildwood (which veers northeast) and then turn right (south) on Butternut Drive, which also has bike paths. Cycle south on Butternut Drive to 144th Avenue where you turn right (west) onto Lakewood Boulevard. Lakewood Boulevard deadends at Lake Shore Avenue where you can head south on the bike path to return to Tunnel Park.

Bicycle sales, service

The Bicycle Shop, 8 N. Ferry St., Grand Haven; (616) 846-5600.

Cross Country Cycle, 137 N. River Ave., Holland; (616) 396-7491.

Highwheeler Bicycle Shop, 211 S. River Ave., Holland; (616) 396-6084.

Holland Schwinn Cyclery, 250 S. River Ave., Holland; (616) 393-0046.

Breakaway Bicycles, 17280 Robbins Rd., Grand Haven; (616) 844-1199.

Rock 'n' Road Cycle, 300 N. Seventh St., Grand Haven; (616) 846-2800.

Zeeland Schwinn Cyclery, 201 E. Main Ave., Zeeland; (616) 772-6223.

Bicycle rental

Karol's Bike Rentals Inc., 1895 Ottawa Beach Rd., Holland; (616) 399-3993.

Area attractions

Dutch Village; (616) 396-1475.

Veldheer Tulip Gardens, DeKlomp Wooden Shoe & Delft-ware Factory; (616) 399-1900.

Windmill Island; (616) 396-5433.

Wooden Shoe Factory; (616) 396-6513.

Musical Fountain, Grand Haven; (616) 842-4499.

Area events and festivals

May: Tulip Time Festival, Holland.

June: Libertyfest, Holland; Sand Sculpture Contest, Grand Haven.

July: Classic Boat Rendezvous, Grand Haven; Up in Central Park Art Show, Grand Haven.

August: Coast Guard Festival, Grand Haven

October: Fall Color Fest, Grand Haven.

Travel information

Holland Area Convention & Visitors Bureau, (616) 396-4221.

Holland Chamber of Commerce; (616) 396-2389.

Grand Haven Association of Commerce & Industry, (616) 842-4910.

Grand Haven/Spring Lake Visitors Bureau, (616) 842-4499.

The Lake Michigan beach at Holland State Park.

The rail bridge along the Kent Trails in Grand Rapids.

9 Kent Trails

TRIP CARD

Starting point: Grand Rapids
County: Kent
Distance: 30 miles round trip
Shorter option: 7 to 10 miles
Terrain: flat, converted rail bed, pipeline, some roads
Highlights: John Ball Park & Zoo, downtown Grand Rapids, Johnson Park, Douglas Walker Park
Suggested riders: beginners

Cyclers! You may
be fantasizing
Tour D'France.

Definitely plan
to Tour D'Sewer
side.

Wake up, It's
Kent County and this
is Tour D'Fence.

Wyoming invites
you to get off
your bicycle

Enjoy your day
and when you
recall this ride,

Call (616) 534-8606
and learn how
to recycle.

This humorous poem greets cyclists heading north on the Kent Trails, a 15-mile trail dedicated in May 1992. So what's the charm of a trail partially fenced-in with (yech!) barbed wire, travels over a new pipeline, and has a repaved road and an old rail trail? It's the fact that you're in Michigan's second largest metropolitan area and that you don't have to worry much about the pitfalls of automobile traffic.

The dream of this trail began in 1986 when the Penn Central Railroad, interested in selling off its old rail line, contacted the Kent County Parks Department. With the help of a Michigan Department of Natural Resources grant, Kent County brought together six governmental bodies (not a small feat!) to make this vision of a single trail connecting three major parks in the Grand Rapids-area a reality.

The trail begins in an urban setting, near a Coca Cola bottling plant, just south of the John Ball Park & Zoo. One nippy Sunday afternoon very early in the cycling season, we ventured onto the path and weren't immediately impressed with the high fences and small patches of barbed wire. But eventually the fence gave way to a winding pathway along the Grand River. We crossed a refurbished bridge, with new aqua-colored paint and fresh cement, yet, we still knew it was a railroad bridge.

And at 1.7 miles into the trip the trail turned to Indian Mounds Road, where between 200 B.C. and 400 A.D. the Hopewellian Indian people created the mounds on the west bank of the Grand River, Michigan's longest river. Throughout the Kent Trails, the aqua-colored posts featuring the trail logo will keep you on track for the whole route.

After journeying 5.4 miles south to the trailhead at Prairie Street in Grandville, the ride turns into what a lot of touring cyclists love - a long, fast, flat, asphalt trail with no more than five percent grade. This segment winds through farmlands, new residential construction, past a golf course and under a bridge. The trail ends at the big white chicken of the Byron Center Hotel, whose sign reads "BAR-chicken dinners every Saturday night." From there it's 2.7 rolling miles on 84th Street to the final destination - Douglas Walker Park. We turned left on 84th Street in Byron Center, locked the bicycles and enjoyed a leisurely lunch of burgers and sandwiches at the Byron Family Restaurant (616-878-1888). This place has a great small-town appeal. After lunch, it was back on the trail for the return trip to John Ball Park & Zoo.

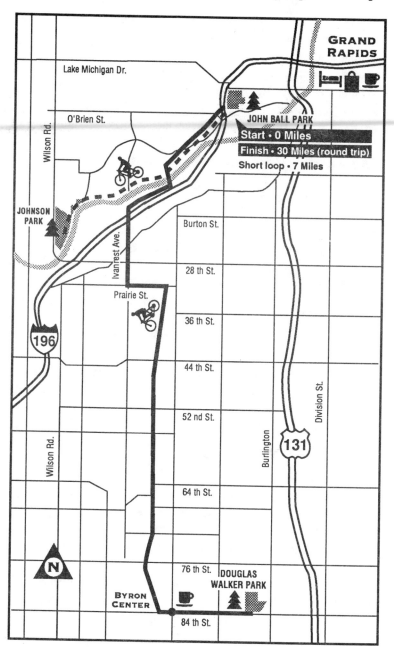

GRAND RAPIDS

Lake Michigan Dr.

O'Brien St.

Wilson Rd.

JOHN BALL PARK

Start • 0 Miles
Finish • 30 Miles (round trip)
Short loop • 7 Miles

JOHNSON PARK

Burton St.

Ivanrest Ave.

28 th St.

Prairie St.

36 th St.

196

44 th St.

52 nd St.

Division St.

Burlington

131

Wilson Rd.

64 th St.

N

76 th St. DOUGLAS WALKER PARK

BYRON CENTER

84 th St.

Grand Rapids is a bustling community known for its downtown fireworks on the Fourth of July, its Celebration on the Grand (an annual event which began when hometown boy- Gerald R. Ford was president), in September and probably the largest, all-volunteer, local arts festival in the world held in June. The festival has been nicknamed "Foodfest" with delicacies such as souvlaki (Greek), elephant ears with cinnamon sugar, kielbasa (Polish) and, new in 1992, Pavlovas (Australian whipped cream and fresh fruit, topped with meringue) and barbecue turkey drumsticks.

If you decide to do 30 miles round trip, your non-cycling friends and family members can ride a shorter loop and enjoy the zoo, eat their hearts out at a festival or in one of the area's hundreds of restaurants, or do some power shopping on 28th Street, Plainfield Avenue or Alpine Avenue (major shoppers' rows). That way everyone's happy, from Mom on down to the baby sister.

The trail is ideal for shorter loops, too. We recommend the 10.2 mile stretch from 44th Street to 84th Street (round trip), or the 7-mile trip (round trip) from the John Ball Park & Zoo to Johnson Park and back.

Stage one (5.4 miles) From John Ball Park & Zoo, head south on the trail near the Coca Cola bottling plant. This is an off-road section over a new pipeline. At 1.7 miles turn left and cross the Grand River on an old, yet refurbished, railroad bridge. Continue south on Indian Mounds Drive for 1.3 miles and then look for the Kent Trails posts that direct you to a short off-road section to Ivanrest Avenue.

Another option, instead of crossing the railroad bridge, is to keep riding on the off-road section over new pipeline and then onto Veterans Memorial Drive to Johnson Park. The 245-acre park is on the Grand River and features picnic facilities, fishing, trails and a playground.

At 3.6 miles you have the unique experience of traveling on a road with a wastewater plant on your left while on the other side is the West Michigan Readi Mix plant and West Michigan Recycled

Aggregate. Talk about natural surroundings. Shortly after that, you arrive at an odd intersection on Ivanrest Avenue with a sharply-angled Chicago Drive. Continue on Ivanrest Avenue but be cautious as this road can have heavy traffic depending on the time of day. Cross 28th Street (busy, busy!) at 4.2 miles to Prairie Street. Take a left on Prairie Street and cycle less than a mile to the beginning of the rail trail. Whew! You made it.

Stage two (5.3 miles) The trail is relaxing and, more important, flat, making enjoyable conversations possible. Cross 36th Street at 5.9 miles and look for the wooden bridge at 6.3 miles. In a half mile, take a left at Spartan Industrial Drive and follow the aqua-colored posts to the trailhead at 44th Street, which along with 36th Street, can be a busy road. But don't despair, from here on the trailhead is a straight line to Byron Center. At 8.2 miles, you'll cross 52nd Street and at 10.7 miles you'll cross 72nd Street.

Stage three (4.3 miles) For the final leg of the Kent Trails, travel 1.6 miles until the end of the rail trail at 84th Street; turn left. This road heads east 2.7 miles over rolling, long hills through downtown Byron Center to Douglas Walker Park. Byron Center is quintessential small-town America with several family restaurants and lots of chances for refreshing ice cream breaks. Another option is to leave the trail and turn left on 76th Street and then travel east for approximately 3 miles. Here 76th Street connects with another off-road bike path that leads south to Douglas Walker Park.

Bicycle sales, service
Alger Schwinn Cycling & Fitness, 120 28th St. SW, Grand Rapids; (616) 243-9753.

Alpine Cyclery, 3150 Alpine Ave. NW, Walker; (616) 785-0505.

Chicago Drive Schwinn Cycling & Fitness, 4300 Chicago Dr. SW, Grandville; (616) 531-9911

Freewheeler Bike Shop, 915 Leonard St. NW, Grand Rapids; (616) 451-8011.

Kentwood Schwinn Cycling & Fitness, 2830 East Paris SE, Kentwood; (616) 942-1880.

North Kent Schwinn, 4318 Plainfield Ave. NE; Grand Rapids; (616) 363-0705.

Progressive Bicycles, 1811 Plainfield Ave. NE, Grand Rapids; (616) 364-3100.

Village Bike Shop, 7642 Riverview Dr., Jenison; (616)457-1670.

Village Bike Shop, 4252 Kalamazoo SE, Grand Rapids; (616) 455-4870.

Area attractions
Blandford Nature Center, Grand Rapids; (616)453-6192.
Fish Ladder and 6th Street Dam on Grand River.
Gerald R. Ford Museum, Grand Rapids, (616) 456-2674.
John Ball Park & Zoo, Grand Rapids; (616) 776-2590.
Public Museum of Grand Rapids; (616) 456-3966.
Splash Water Park, Grand Rapids; (616) 940-3100.

Area events and festivals
May: Old Kent River Bank Run, Grand Rapids.
June: Festival of the Arts, Grand Rapids.
September: Celebration on the Grand, Grand Rapids.
October: Pulaski Days, Grand Rapids.

Travel Information
Grand Rapids/Kent County Convention & Visitors Bureau, (616) 459-8287.

Grand Rapids Area Chamber of Commerce (616) 771-0300.
Kent County Park Commission (616) 774-3697.
West Michigan Tourist Association (616)456-8557.

10 Apple Country

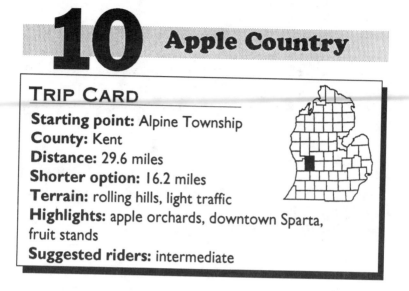

TRIP CARD

Starting point: Alpine Township
County: Kent
Distance: 29.6 miles
Shorter option: 16.2 miles
Terrain: rolling hills, light traffic
Highlights: apple orchards, downtown Sparta, fruit stands
Suggested riders: intermediate

"The Ridge", a little-known area in the northwest portion of Kent County and a part of Ottawa County, is blessed with hilly terrain and the proper distance from Lake Michigan that makes an ideal apple growing climate. It's the main reason Kent County grows more apples than any other county in Michigan. Rolling hills and scenic orchards also make this route a cyclist's dream.

From the days of annual apple smorgasbords which attracted national food writers, and 40 years of apple queens, the region is rich in tradition and loaded with apples. Today, the apple queens and smorgasbords may be gone but the bountiful apple harvest is still around and every fall people bite into such varieties as Ida Red, Macintosh, Jonathan, Delicious, Golden Delicious, Rome, Northern Spy, Wine Sap and Granny Smith along with little-known apples like Fugi and Gala. Harvesting the orchards is a group of down-to-earth friendly folk, who have a passion for the land. It's not uncommon for a fifth-generation apple grower to be managing the family orchards.

Bicyclists will delight in this refreshing 29.6-mile journey that

93

Apple trees seen from the bike route in Alpine Township.

winds through the heart of apple country and past a half-dozen centennial farms. The ride begins appropriately at the Alpine Township Hall, on Alpine Avenue, northwest of Grand Rapids. Early May is an ideal time to journey through apple country as the blossoms are on the verge of bursting and often the temperature will be a comfortable mid-60s with slight breezes cooling you off at the top of the hills. Hills??? The beauty of these hills is that most of the time you'll have enough forward momentum going down to get you back up the next one. There's only one "thigh-burner", on Baumhoff Avenue coming back, but what's a ride without at least one hard, steep hill to help work up a good appetite.

Over halfway through the ride, you'll end up in downtown Sparta, a town of over 3,300 residents. Sparta is far enough (15 miles) away from the Grand Rapids metropolitan area to have its own identity and atmosphere. There's a couple of restaurants here, Cnossen's and Rosita's Mexican Cafe, that will give you a feel for the local color. On your way out of Sparta, there's a fruit and vegetable stand, Bergman's, just one of many fruit stands and U-pick farms in the area. The Bergmans began selling fruit from their front porch in the 1930's.

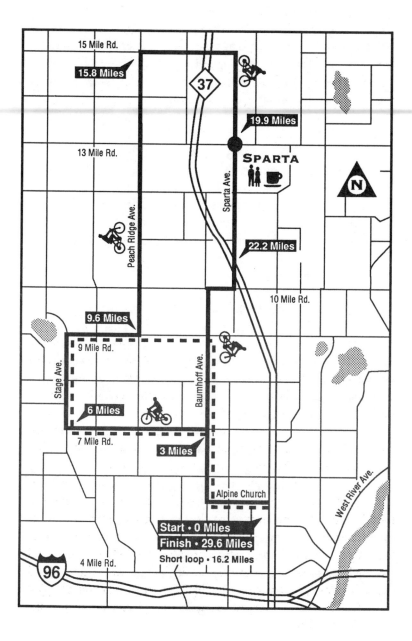

15 Mile Rd.

15.8 Miles

37

19.9 Miles

13 Mile Rd.

SPARTA

Sparta Ave.

Peach Ridge Ave.

N

22.2 Miles

10 Mile Rd.

9.6 Miles

9 Mile Rd.

Baumhoff Ave.

Stage Ave.

6 Miles

7 Mile Rd.

3 Miles

Alpine Church

West River Ave.

Start • 0 Miles
Finish • 29.6 Miles
Short loop • 16.2 Miles

96

4 Mile Rd.

You'll keep the power shopper in your group happy with this tour. Before or after your ride, you and your family can shop on Alpine Avenue, a strip that's become a mega-store area for discount and bargain shopping. Of course, there are restaurants here as well; Village Inn Pizza, Mr. Fables, Dairy Queen while hundreds more are not that far away in the greater Grand Rapids area.

Stage one (8.1 miles) Park in the Alpine Township Hall parking lot at 841 Alpine Church Rd., on the corner of Alpine Avenue (M-37) and Alpine Church Road. Head west on Alpine Church Road and in 1.5 miles turn right (north) on Baumhoff Avenue and pedal north until you reach 7 Mile Road at 3 miles. Turn left (west) on 7 Mile Road and shortly you'll pass the Alpine Historic Township Hall and Museum (616-785-0205). It's open the third Sunday of each month for those who want to step back into the history of this apple-growing region.

Continue west on 7 Mile Road and at 6 miles turn right (north) onto Stage Avenue. Stage Avenue is a scenic stretch with woodlots to the west and orchards so close on the right you can practically pick a bushel while pedaling through. Before heading east on 9 Mile Road, you can take a break by staying on Stage Avenue which quickly swings past Cranberry Lake, a small lake, half in Ottawa County and half in Kent County.

Stage Two (7.7 miles) From Stage Avenue, turn right (east) on 9 Mile Road and travel for 1.5 miles and then turn left (north) on Peach Ridge Avenue at 9.6 miles. Until the late 1920s, farmers grew a lot of peaches in this area, now it's mostly apples and a few scattered peach trees, but the name of the road remained. On Peach Ridge Avenue, you head north for 6 miles. Unlike most lakeshore routes, the roads on the Apple Country Tour are straight, laid out in true directions of a compass. Roads such a 7, 9 and 15 Mile Roads make it easy for cyclists to know how far they have gone. Others; Apple Ridge, Peach Ridge and Fruit Ridge,

Cycling past apple orchards in bloom in Alpine Township.
remind you where you are.

Stage Three (4.1 miles) From Peach Ridge Avenue, turn right on 15 Mile Road, at 15.8 miles, and journey for 2 miles to Sparta Avenue. Turn right on Sparta Avenue and it's 2 more miles into downtown Sparta. This is the portion of the route with the most traffic, although it's lighter on weekends. Sparta is a town with a mix of old and new neighborhoods and its share of small industry. But apples are what Sparta is best known for and what the town actively promotes.

Stage four (9.7 miles) Head south out of Sparta on Sparta Avenue to M-37 (Alpine Avenue). M-37 is often a busy highway that has to be carefully crossed to reach 10 Mile Road on the west side. Head right (west) on 10 Mile Road and in less than a mile you'll reach a picturesque Church of Christ at Ballard's Corner. Turn left (south) on Baumhoff Avenue to end the day with a rolling 5-mile ride back to Alpine Church Road.   Beware: there's one "thigh-burner" on this final stretch. From Baumhoff Avenue, turn left (east) on Alpine Church Street to return to the starting point at the Alpine Township Hall. You will pass Holy Trinity Catholic Church, nestled in a pretty (spiritual?) setting on your right, with a quiet cemetery across the road.

Shorter option For a shorter 16-mile loop, cycle west on Alpine Church Street and turn right (north) on Baumhoff Avenue. Turn left (west) on 7 Mile Road and then head right (north) on Stage Avenue. Cycle to 9 Mile Road and turn right (east). But instead of heading north on Peach Ridge Avenue, continue on 9 Mile Road to Baumhoff Avenue. Turn right (south) on Baumhoff Avenue to Alpine Church Street and a quicker return to the starting point at the Alpine Township Hall.

Bicycle sales, service
Freewheeler Bike Shop, 915 Leonard St. NW, Grand Rapids; (616) 451-8011.

Alpine Cyclery, 3150 Alpine Ave. NW, Walker; (616) 785-0505.

North Kent Schwinn, 4318 Plainfield Ave. NE; Grand Rapids; (616) 363-0705.

Area events and festivals
June: Grand Rapids Festival of the Arts.

July: Sparta Town & Country Days.

September: Celebration on the Grand, Grand Rapids; Klein Rodeo, Sparta.

October: Pulaski Days, Grand Rapids.

Travel information
Sparta Area Chamber of Commerce; (616)887-2454.

Grand Rapids/Kent County Convention & Visitors Bureau; (616) 459-8287.

Grand Rapids Area Chamber of Commerce; (616) 771-0300.

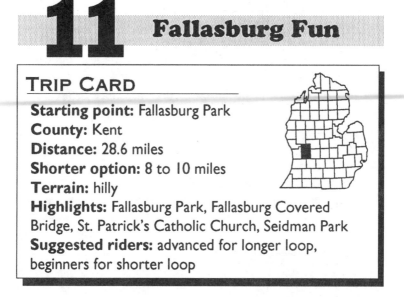

11 Fallasburg Fun

TRIP CARD

Starting point: Fallasburg Park
County: Kent
Distance: 28.6 miles
Shorter option: 8 to 10 miles
Terrain: hilly
Highlights: Fallasburg Park, Fallasburg Covered Bridge, St. Patrick's Catholic Church, Seidman Park
Suggested riders: advanced for longer loop, beginners for shorter loop

Fallasburg Park, located north of Lowell in Kent County, is an ideal starting point for a bike ride. Known best for its historical covered bridge, the park is appropriately named because fall is the most spectacular time of year to visit the area. You not only get to enjoy the changing colors but you can also participate in the many events staged during autumn.

Riders of varying abilities will enjoy the 458-acre park which has fishing, nature trails and play equipment. Beginning cyclists may want to just ride the short distance to Lowell and back and then wait at one of the many scenic picnic spots while others grind out the 28.5 loop. This longer circuit heads north out of the park, works its way east to Parnell, then south to Ada before looping back to the park. On this jaunt you'll enjoy an excellent workout and wonderful scenery which will soothe your city-frazzled nerves. The latter half of the loop is particularly hilly with hills that roll and wind and don't want to level out by any means!

The highlight of the tour is the Fallasburg Historic Covered Bridge. Built in 1871 for $1,500, the bridge is undoubtedly the most photographed in the state. The long wooden structure is used each year in late June as part of the Multiple Sclerosis Bikeathon from Grand Rapids to Lansing. The bikeathon is a beautiful sight - hundreds of brightly-clad cyclists journeying over the wooden bridge. Across from the bridge is the Fallasburg Schoolhouse Museum. The country school, built in the 1860's, is open weekends from Memorial Day to mid-October.

Just five miles away near Smyrna, but not a part of this circuit, is White's Bridge. Built in 1867, this covered bridge also spans the Flat River. Also nearby, but not on the bike loop, is the Ada Covered Bridge which crosses the Thornapple River in Ada. This bridge, for pedestrians only, was built in 1867 and rebuilt in 1980 after a fire burned the original structure.

The countryside on this stretch is beautiful with many convenient places to stop. More than half the loop is a county-designated bicycle route, featuring wide shoulders. There are a couple of small stores with bathroom facilities, and places for refreshments on Parnell Road. When we toured the area, we stopped and admired the stately St. Patrick's Catholic Church, a centennial building that was built in 1877. Its steeple is visible for miles and can be seen while traveling west on Parnell Road.

There are also two parks and lakes where you can stop and rest and admire the beauty; Townsend Park, 13.1 miles into the loop, and Seidman Park at 17.3 miles. Only 20 miles from Grand Rapids, Lowell is renowned for its Showboat on the Flat River, an event held the third weekend in June featuring nationally known entertainers. The Flat River Antique Mall, in downtown Lowell, includes four floors of antiques and collectibles and it's open on Sundays too, making it a wonderful place to browse before or after your ride. It's rated as the best mall in the Glovebox Guidebook's *Michigan's Only Antique and Flea Market Guide*. In Lowell there are also many places for the hungry cyclist to eat, ranging from fast food chain restaurants to the West Side Deli.

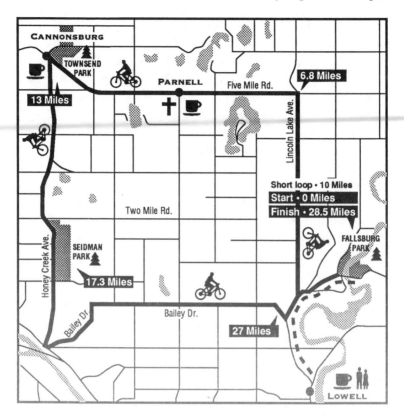

Stage one (9.9 miles) From Fallasburg Covered Bridge in Fallasburg Park, head west on Covered Bridge Road to Lincoln Lake Avenue where you turn right (north). By starting at the bridge, the first 2 miles is a scenic jaunt along the park drive. Heading north on Lincoln Lake Avenue, you'll discover this road is relatively flat with nice wide shoulders and light traffic. At 6.8 miles, turn left (west) on Parnell Road, also labeled 5 Mile Road. Both Lincoln Lake Avenue and Parnell Road are a designated county bike route. At 9.9 miles, there's a small store across from the stately St. Patrick's Catholic Church and cemetery on Parnell Road. This is a leisurely place to take a refreshment break and savor the countryside. Remember to drink lots of liquids.

Stage two (9.5 miles) Keep heading west on Parnell Road which veers northwest and turns into Cannonsburg Road, still part of the designated bike route. At 13.1 miles, on the corner of Cannonsburg Road and Honey Creek Avenue, there's Donahue's Corner Market and the Honey Creek Inn, a quaint country bar and restaurant with imported beer on tap (in case anybody is still hungry from the last break) while just to the north is Townsend Park. This 157-acre county park has plenty of opportunities for fishing and hiking along the nature trails. From the park, head south on Honey Creek Avenue. Within a mile you return to a designated bike route. At 17.3 miles, there's Seidman Park, a 422-acre unit with opportunities for hikers and anglers as well as cross country skiers in the winter. In a route of hilly terrain, there is one heart-pounding hill located at the end of stage two. Suck in a deep breath, put your head down and climb!

Stage three (9.2 miles) From Honey Creek Avenue, turn left on Pettis Avenue and then make another quick left on Vergennes Street and immediately look for Bailey Drive, which veers off to the northeast. This is an odd intersection with four streets coming together by the Grand River. Shady Acres Farms, reached at 23.9 miles, offers hayrides in a rustic country setting. Bailey Road winds past homes in picturesque settings as you tour 8.4 miles back to your final destination at Fallasburg Park. At 27 miles, turn left (north) on Lincoln Lake Avenue and then right (east) on Fallasburg Park Drive to re-enter the park. Whew! Time to relax in the park, take pictures by the covered bridge, grill your dinner or head to Lowell to a local restaurant.

Shorter option Cycle through Fallasburg Park and then turn left (south) on Lincoln Lake Avenue. From the entrance of the park, it's approximately four miles to the town of Lowell. You can cycle as far into town as you want to go before backtracking to the park.

Area events and festivals
June: Lowell Showboat, Lowell; (800-422-SHOW),

Cycling across the Fallasburg Covered Bridge.

(616) 897-8280.

August: Kent County Youth Fair, Lowell fairgrounds; Sunsplash at Fallasburg Park (reggae music).

September: Alto Fall Festival, Alto; Fallasburg Fall Festival, Fallasburg Park.

Travel information

Lowell Area Chamber of Commerce; (616) 897-9161.

Cyclist on the Rockford Dam at the Rogue River.

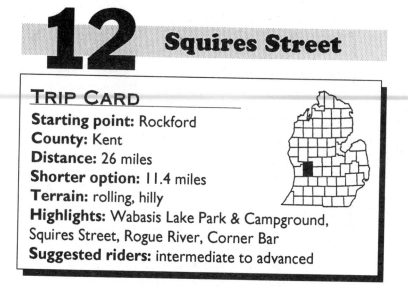

12 **Squires Street**

TRIP CARD

Starting point: Rockford
County: Kent
Distance: 26 miles
Shorter option: 11.4 miles
Terrain: rolling, hilly
Highlights: Wabasis Lake Park & Campground, Squires Street, Rogue River, Corner Bar
Suggested riders: intermediate to advanced

If you're looking for a miniature ceramic collie, a half pound of fresh-roasted coffee, quality second-hand clothing, baskets of all shapes and sizes, humorous birthday cards or hanging crystals for your window, you'll find it at the Squires Street Square, a diverse shopping area in downtown Rockford. This quaint town of 3,000 residents is 15 miles north of Grand Rapids and known as a shopper's paradise. But historical Rockford also serves as a good home base for a 26-mile bicycle route with an optional 11.4-mile loop.

Rockford was founded in 1843 when a young entrepreneur named Smith Lapham purchased land along the Rogue River and then built a dam and saw mill. A shingle mill, grist mill and machine shop soon followed and by the late 1800s Rockford was a bustling commercial center with warehouses, train depot, and a bean processing plant on the river.

The town then experienced a rebirth in the early 1970s when the bean warehouse was renovated into a cider mill, attracting both locals and visitors heading north. Eventually the sweet cider and even sweeter donuts of the Old Mill lead to the shopping district of Squires Street Square, where today you'll find unique shops while nearby is west Michigan's first outlet mall and the factory store of Wolverine World Wide, maker of Hush Puppies shoes.

This 26-mile bicycle route begins in the Squires Street area near the dam, an ideal resting place before or after your ride, where anglers can often be seen casting for steelhead and salmon. The route is a hilly, sometimes winding ride, through a mixture of open country, farms and stands of hardwoods. Wabasis Lake Park and Campground, at mile 10 of the tour, is an impressive area with a large shimmering lake. It is managed by the Kent County Parks Department and features a full-service campground, a beach, bathhouses, and a youth hostel for inexpensive lodging. The park itself is quite hilly; so if you venture into it, be prepared to climb a couple of hills back out.

The return to Rockford on Summit Avenue is a fun, winding, downhill ride while the 11.4-mile loop option provides a taste of the surrounding area as well as the opportunity to cycle past two small lakes; Brower and Myers.

To motivate yourself up those lengthy hills along the loop, keep in mind the many fine eateries with a fresh table waiting for you at the finish in Rockford. Probably the most famous is the Corner Bar, 31 North Main St. (616-866-9866). Since 1965, the Corner Bar has not only been serving great hot dogs but is the site of the Hot Dog Hall of Fame. If you eat 12 hot dogs in four hours or less, you too can be inducted into this hall with your name engraved onto a brass plate on the wall. If you're seeking gastronomic fame, I recommend you try after your bike ride, not before. By the way, the record is 42 1/2 chili dogs consumed in a single sitting and is held by...Sharon Scholten.

There are many other fine restaurants in Rockford, including a Grand Rapids favorite, Vitale's Pizza, 42 E. Bridge St., (616-866-4467), and Arnie's Old Mill Restaurant, 31 Squires St., (616-866-4306).

Stage one (9.9 miles) The starting point is a parking area

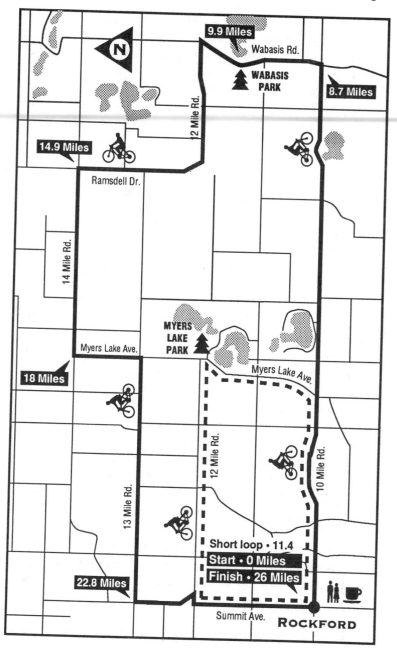

on East Bridge Street, near the Squires Street shops and the Rogue River dam. Turn left on East Bridge Street and then right on South Main Street, where Speed Merchants Bike Shop is on this corner for any last minute repairs. Turn left on East Division and head east out of town on 10 Mile Road where you'll soon pass a McDonalds restaurant (time to eat yet??)

This is a cardiovascular ride and you're tipped off to this by some steep hills early in the tour. A long hill is encountered at 1.9 miles and another after passing Myers Lake Avenue at 3.4 miles. Big Brower Lake will be seen to the north and then Ramsdell Drive at 6.4 miles. At 8.7 miles turn left (north) on Wabasis Avenue and look to your right at 9.9 miles for the Wabasis Lake Park.

The 102-acre park is located on the west side of its namesake lake and features several picnic areas with shelters, restrooms, water, a bathhouse, swimming beach and a small store in the campground. This is a good place to check out the activity on the lake, stretch your legs or munch on some treats you've packed.

Stage two (9.2 miles) From the entrance to Wabasis Park, head north again on Wabasis Avenue where you immediately pass a parking lot for a scenic overlook above the lake. Turn left (west) onto 12 Mile Road at 10.9 miles and in 2 miles turn right (north) on Ramsdell Drive. After crossing Peterson Street at 13.4 miles, turn left (west) on 14 Mile Road (M-57) at 14.9 miles. This can be a busy highway, so another option is to turn left (west) earlier on Peterson Street, though this would shorten the ride by 3 miles. Follow M-57 for 3 miles then turn left (south) onto Myers Lake Avenue to reach 13 Mile Road within a mile to complete stage two and 19 miles of the tour.

Stage three (7 miles) Head west on 13 Mile Road for 4 miles and then turn left (south) on Summit Avenue at 22.8 miles. Within a mile you'll arrive at a quirky intersection where you turn right (west) on 12 Mile Road and then make an immediate left (south) back onto Summit Avenue.

The final leg is a scenic and roguish stretch. You'll be cycling parallel to the Rogue River while descending back to the downtown area. At 25.2 miles, the Rockford city limits is reached. Cross the river and turn left on Bridge Street to return to the starting point. It's time to browse for distinctive gifts and eat, or simply relax on the banks of the charming Rogue River, watching the canoeists or fishermen.

Shorter option (11.4-mile) From 10 Mile Road, turn left (north) on Myers Lake Avenue to 12 Mile Road, where you turn left (west). Pedal 4 miles on 12 Mile Road to Summit Avenue where you turn left (south) to return to the starting point on East Bridge Street.

Bicycle sales, service
The Speed Merchants, 106 E. Bridge St., Rockford; (616) 866-2226.

Area events and festivals
June: Start of Summer Festival, Rockford.
July: Old Fashioned Sidewalk Sales, Rockford.
September: Harvest Festival, Rockford (three weekends in September and October); Red Flannel Festival, Cedar Springs.

Travel information
Rockford Chamber of Commerce; (616) 866-2000.
Cedar Springs Chamber of Commerce; (616) 696-3260.

The Lake Michigan beach at Duck Lake State Park.

13 Blockhouse Hill

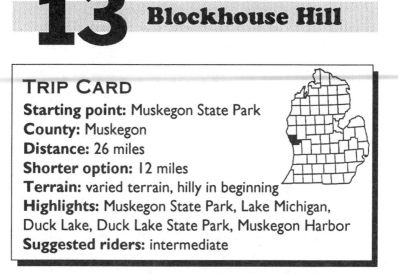

TRIP CARD
Starting point: Muskegon State Park
County: Muskegon
Distance: 26 miles
Shorter option: 12 miles
Terrain: varied terrain, hilly in beginning
Highlights: Muskegon State Park, Lake Michigan, Duck Lake, Duck Lake State Park, Muskegon Harbor
Suggested riders: intermediate

Two large state parks and a county park bordering Lake Michigan, a quaint lakeshore community and a city lined with the mansions of 19th century lumber barons equates, as far as cyclists are concerned, into an area of natural beauty and year-round activities. That's what can be found along a 26-mile route that begins at Muskegon State Park, heads north to Duck Lake State Park on the south side of Whitehall, and ends up back at the state park, on the edge of Muskegon.

Muskegon is blessed with another state park on its south side, P.J. Hoffmaster, known best for the Michigan Sand Dune Interpretive Center. But this bicycle route begins at Muskegon State Park, an equally impressive park just north of town. The loop, made up of lightly traveled roads and beautiful Lake Michigan scenery, offers plenty of opportunities to stop for quick swims and gourmet picnicking.

Don't panic during the first part of the loop; it's very hilly as you make your way out of Muskegon State Park along Scenic Drive. But the effort is definitely worth it, especially when you pause on top of Blockhouse hill, where you can take in a panorama of the park's wooded interior, the dunes along Lake Michigan and even Muskegon Lake. The route becomes easier after the first stage as you follow Lake Michigan to Duck Lake. Along the way you pass by out-of-the-way beaches, a family resort in Michillinda Beach Lodge near Whitehall and delightful cycling roads such as Michillinda Drive.

I pedaled this route on a day when temperatures were in the 80's. Yet I found the ride pleasant because the breezes off of Lake Michigan and the shady segments of the route compensated for the not-so-comfortable heat. The 12.1-mile option allows cyclists to see the lakeshore scenery as well as put in a good, short workout.

This Muskegon-Duck Lake circuit could be the first half of an excellent two-day outing with the second day spent pedaling the 22-mile Hart-Montague Bike Trail, Michigan's first linear state park. The rail-to-trail route (see page 125), begins in Montague, just 15 miles north of Muskegon.

To many, Muskegon is known as an industrial city on the lake, but in recent years tourism has taken on increased importance. There are many family attractions, including Michigan Adventure (616-766-3377), a water and amusement park north of town, and Pleasure Island (616-798-7857), one of the largest water parks in the state (try the 5-second thrill through the park's Black Hole!), along with the state and county parks. Other Muskegon attractions include the Hackley and Hume Homes, restored lumber baron mansions, tours on the USS Silversides, a World War II submarine, and the Port City Cruise Line, offering dinner and scenic cruises.

Fifteen miles north of the area are Muskegon's smaller cousins, Whitehall and Montague, pleasant resort communities on White Lake. There's some neat options for dining here, such as the Crosswinds Restaruant on White Lake. Along the route there are some excellent ice cream stops, or you can grill your dinner back at the state park. The Bear Lake Inn, featuring a fun, casual atmosphere in North Muskegon near the start of the bike route, is also a good place to eat.

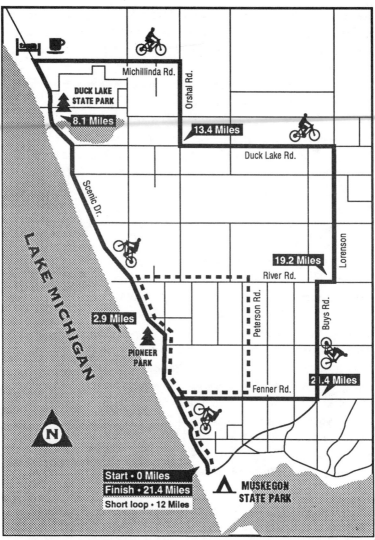

On the map:
- Michillinda Rd.
- Orshal Rd.
- DUCK LAKE STATE PARK
- 8.1 Miles
- 13.4 Miles
- Duck Lake Rd.
- Scenic Dr.
- LAKE MICHIGAN
- Lorenson
- 19.2 Miles
- River Rd.
- Peterson Rd.
- Buys Rd.
- 2.9 Miles
- PIONEER PARK
- Fenner Rd.
- 21.4 Miles
- N
- Start · 0 Miles
- Finish · 21.4 Miles
- Short loop · 12 Miles
- MUSKEGON STATE PARK

Stage one (9.2 miles) From the beach parking area in Muskegon State Park, head north on Scenic Drive. Oh, the hills! But the view makes it worth the effort especially when you reach the The Blockhouse halfway through the park. The original Blockhouse was built by the CCC in 1935 but burned down in 1962. The replica was constructed two years later and from its second floor you can see the park's highpoint, a wooded dune at 792 feet, while to the west is the blue horizon of Lake Michigan and to the southeast Muskegon Lake.

At 2 miles, you'll depart the park and enter a shady neighborhood with Lake Michigan to the west. Cross Giles Road at 2.7 miles, a slightly busy corner, and within a quarter mile you'll reach Pioneer County Park, a popular area for camping and sunbathing. The Red Rooster Tavern is passed at 5.6 miles and is followed by a long stretch of shaded road where the lake breezes provide a comfortable break from the summer heat. There's a small township park to the west at 7.5 miles that provides more access to the beach.

At 8.1 miles you reach a interesting passage between two bodies of water. On your right is Duck Lake with a boardwalk leading to a inland beach and picnic area. On your left is Lake Michigan with another beach beneath a towering dune. Both are part of Duck Lake State Park, a 728-acre unit that was dedicated in 1988. The park is a day-use facility with no campground but arrive on a Saturday in July and you'll be impressed by the dune...and the large number of people spread out on the beach. At 8.9 miles you pass the Michillinda Beach Lodge, an old-fashioned resort with a modified American Plan (some meals, lodging, and use of all facilities included in one price) on Lake Michigan as well as a party store, where you can take a refreshment break. At 9.2 miles, turn right (east) on Michillinda Drive.

Stage two (9.8 miles) Head east on Michillinda Drive and at 10.3 miles you'll pass the entrance of Duck Lake State Park. You'll certainly appreciate the wide shoulders on this road before turning right (south) on Orshal Road at 11.9 miles. A long uphill segment is encountered at 12.8 miles while at 13.4 miles you turn left (east) on Duck Lake Road. Cycle 3.1 miles and then turn right (south) on Lorenson Road. This road features open farm country with some picturesque barns. The second stage ends by turning right (west) on River Road.

The Blockhouse in Muskegon State Park.

Stage three (7 miles) After turning on River Road, you immediately turn left (south) on Buys Road at 19.2 miles. Within a mile you reach the Maple Ridge Historic School, a one-room structure. Turn right at 21.4 miles onto Fenner Road which will lead back into the Muskegon State Park. The Blockhouse is on your left at 25.1 miles, if you didn't stop there on your way out. The ride ends at 26 miles in the middle of the Muskegon State Park.

Shorter option (12.1 miles) Take Scenic Drive north for 4.4 miles and turn right (east) onto River Road. At 6.8 miles turn right on Peterson Road, a lightly traveled road with no shoulders. Cycle to Fenner Road (9.1 miles) and then turn right (west) to reach Scenic Road. Turn left (south) and you'll reach the starting point at the day-use area and beach in the center of the park.

Bicycle sales, service

The Bicycle Rack, 1790 Roberts, Muskegon; (616) 773-6411.

Breakaway Bicycles, 2145 W. Sherman Blvd., Muskegon; (616) 759-0001.

Great Lakes Bicycle Shop, 76 E. Broadway Ave., Muskegon; (616) 733-0906.

Smalligan's Schwinn Bicycles, 1204 S. Getty St., Muskegon; (616) 722-2337.

Rock 'N' Road Cycle, 300 N. 7th, Grand Haven; (616) 846-2800.

Area events and festivals

May: Trillium Festival, Hoffmaster State Park.

June: Lumbertown Festival, Muskegon; White Lake Area Arts and Crafts Festival, Whitehall.

August: White Lake Maritime Festival, Whitehall.

Travel information

Muskegon County Convention & Visitors Bureau, (616) 722-3751.

White Lake Area Chamber of Commerce, (616) 893-4585.

Muskegon State Park, (616) 744-3480.

14 Silver Lake Amble

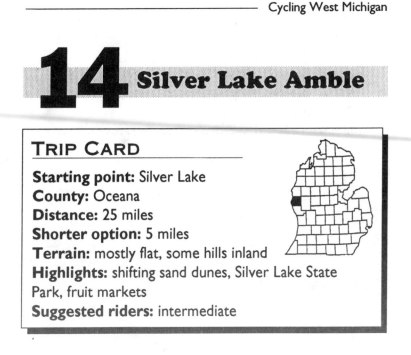

TRIP CARD

Starting point: Silver Lake
County: Oceana
Distance: 25 miles
Shorter option: 5 miles
Terrain: mostly flat, some hills inland
Highlights: shifting sand dunes, Silver Lake State Park, fruit markets
Suggested riders: intermediate

They call the dunes of Silver Lake State Park Michigan's own Sahara Desert. The 2,800-acre unit is another Lake Michigan park with 1,800 acres of it forming a mile-wide strip between the Great Lake and Silver Lake. Even for the dune country of west Michigan this area is unique. Its ridges and valleys are mostly wind-blown sand, lacking trees, scrub, even dune grass to form steep-side mountains of shifting sand.

The dunes, the park and all the side attractions of the area, ranging from dune buggy rides to water slides, attracts hordes of visitors every summer. But the area also makes a logical starting point for a pleasant 25-mile cycling route, that begins at Silver Lake State Park. The ride heads south out of the hustle and bustle of tourists and away from the strips of restaurants, resorts and campgrounds and quickly takes you into open farm and orchard country.

You'll quickly discover on this ride that Oceana County is a major fruit and vegetable-growing area. More tart cherries are

Silver Lake and the famous Silver Lake sand dunes.

grown here than any other county in the United States, including Grand Traverse County, Michigan's so-called cherry country. Then there is the asparagus! There's so much grown here that the towns of Hart and Shelby put on an annual Asparagus Festival that is highlighted with the crowning of the Asparagus Queen. I'm not kidding.

There's the Cherry Point Farm Market, reached at mile 4 of the tour, for a wide range of cherry and fruit products, and then the ride heads east, close to Shelby before looping back through Mears and the Silver Lake area.

This Silver Lake loop could also be easily combined with the 22-mile Hart-Montague Trail (see page 125) for a longer ride or a weekend of cycling, as this route intersects the Hart-Montague Trail at two different points.

Those with extra time before or after the ride will enjoy the natural features of Silver Lake State Park. The dunes have been divided into three separate areas with small sections at the north end designated for ORVs and the south end for a dune-ride concession. Mac Wood's Dune Rides (616-873-2817) offers rides

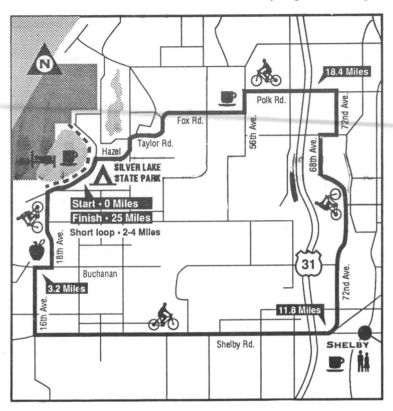

on 12-passenger open truck-like "dune scooters." The Wood family has been riding the sands for over 60 years, entertaining visitors with a bit of history and folklore, while zigzagging up, over and around the dunes.

The majority of the dunes in the middle is a pedestrian area. Here visitors depart their cars (or bicycles) and take to the Sahara Desert on foot in a mile-long trek to the beautiful and uncrowded beaches along Lake Michigan. Equally interesting is the Little Point Sable Lighthouse at the south end of the park. Built in 1874, the lighthouse is still maintained by the Coast Guard but is best known as one of the most scenic places to watch a sunset over Lake Michigan. The lighthouse day-use area is reached by continuing west where Scenic Drive (also County Road B15) turns south at the Mac Woods Dune Rides and following the signs along the narrow dirt road, perfect on a mountain bike.

Of course any place that attracts this many summer tourists, must serve ice cream by the ton...one scoop at a time. Overheated cyclists will appreciate several places on "the strip", including Whippy Dip (home of the famous turtle sundae) near the state park and soft and hard ice cream at the Sands Restaurant.

Stage one (3.2 miles) From Silver Lake State Park, head south on Scenic Drive but be careful; the road can be very busy with cars, pedestrians and bike traffic. You'll pass by cottages on both sides and Flora-dale Resort, a lively family resort. Within a mile the road curves to the left (south) as 18th Avenue and on the corner is Mac Wood's Dune Rides followed by the Whippy Dip. For those on mountain bikes, you can continue straight for a side trip to the lighthouse, an extra 3 miles at this point. Little Sable Point Lighthouse is one of the most photographed in the state even though the adjoining lightkeeper's house was demolished in 1954, leaving only the conical tower. But at 108 feet in height, it's one of the tallest on the west side of the state and requires 145 steps to reach the lens at the top.

The tour, meanwhile, heads south on 18th Avenue (also labeled County Road B15 on maps), a fairly wide road that is lightly travelled. You pass through farm country and apple orchards and pedal segments that are lined by ancient oaks or maples and painted in early summer by wildflowers. At 2.9 miles 18th Avenue curves to the right (west) and merges into Buchanan Road at this point. More orchards are passed and at 3.2 miles Cherry Point Farm Market is reached. Snack time! The market is open seven days a week, selling homemade cherry pies, bread, baked goods, jams and jelly, hot or cold drinks as well as a selection of country crafts and gifts. It's a friendly place to stop for a quick break or load up your bike bag with snacks for later.

Stage two (11.3 miles) From Cherry Point Farm Market, the road curves sharply to your left (south) and becomes 16th

Avenue, (still called Scenic Drive and County Road B15). You'll struggle over a hill at 4.4 miles and then within a third mile turn left (east) on Shelby Road. Shelby Road is a pleasant mixture of stands of pines and hardwoods, faded red barns, wildflowers and orchards. There's a long, but gradual uphill section beginning at 7.1 miles followed by more fertile orchards and trees. In the next 2 miles you'll cycle past a slice of rural Michigan; including large wooden barns and silos and a centennial farm with a bulky stone porch.

A hilly section is encountered At 9.5 miles before the road levels out and you eventually cross the US-31 overpass. At 11.8 miles turn left (north) on 72nd Street, located just west of the town of Shelby. This road immediately heads downhill, curving to the right and is a narrow but lightly traveled avenue. You pass horse stables and encounter more hills, including a steep one at 12.5 miles reached just before you intersect the Hart-Montague Trail. Stay on 72nd Avenue and guess what? More orchards and hills! This stretch is the most rolling portion of the Silver Lake route and begins with a steep incline at 13.9 miles followed by an equally long downhill ride (ahhhhh!) at 14.4 miles. You'll pass Baseline Road at 14.5 miles to complete stage two.

Stage three (10.5 miles) Just north of Baseline Road, 72nd Avenue becomes a well, shaded route and then at 14.9 miles swings west to skirt around Crystal Lake, a small lake with a few cottages. Just after Scout Road merges from the east, there's a public access site on the lake, a pleasant spot if your tired legs need a break.

At Crystal Lake the road turns into 68th Avenue and is followed by another long, steep hill, past Duck Road, at 15.3 miles. Straight ahead you come to the junction and stop sign on Taylor Road where nearby a dilapidated church sits. Swing right (east) on Taylor and then left (north) back on 72nd Avenue where a gradual hill is encountered at 16.8 followed by a mix of hardwoods and orchards that pleasantly line the road.

You intersect the Hart-Montague Trail again at 17.5 miles just

Little Point Sable Lighthouse in Silver Lake State Park.

before turning left (west) on Polk Road. This is a busy road, but features wide shoulders on both sides. Within a half mile you'll pass over US-31 a second time and then head due west as Polk Road narrows down to two lanes. Turn left (south) on 56th Avenue at 19.6 miles and then right (west) in a half mile on 4th Avenue (also called Hazel Road). Soon you'll enter the small town of Mears, a good place to stop for a breather before returning to Silver Lake.

Named after a west Michigan lumber baron, Mears has a grocery store, restaurant and antique shops. It's also the home of the Mears Newz bulletin board that is changed on a regular basis by local citizens. Residents invite you to stop and check out "What's ripe in the Land of Mears!" The Oceana County Museum in Mears was once the home of Swift Lathers, who published the Mears Newz for more than 50 years as the world's smallest newspaper. Just south of the town, the Hart-Montague Trail passes by.

From Mears, Fox Road heads west to the Silver Lake area, passing through a tunnel of trees at 21.8 miles and another farmer's market at 23.1 miles. In another quarter mile you reach the junction and stop sign at County Road B15. Turn left (south) and you'll quickly notice the brown and white Oceana Circle Tour signs that complement the Lake Michigan Circle Tour signs on federal and state highways. CR-B15 curves sharply to your right at 23.6 miles followed by another right-hand curve as it enters the Silver Lake area curving again to the right. You can see water straight ahead at 23.9 miles. You will also see the flashing neon signs advertising for restaurants, miniature golf, T-shirt shops, ice cream parlours, campgrounds and other tourist trappings before you reach your starting point, the entrance of the Silver Lake State Park at 25 miles.

Shorter option (2-4 miles) The road following Silver Lake has bike route signs and is a leisurely ride for beginners or cyclists who want an off-day. The portion of the road on the north side of Silver Lake is especially nice, with less congestion and ample shoulders. You can cycle as far as you want to go and then backtrack to your motel room or campground.

Note: This 25-mile route can be easily lengthened by cycling further east on Shelby Road into Shelby and cycling further north to Hart before heading back west to Silver Lake. Also keep in mind that to the north, Pentwater (a Silver Lake with more class), is a worthwhile destination. This popular resort town has a state park, many eateries and unique shops. Pentwater can be reached from Silver Lake by heading north on Hazel Road to Ridge Avenue, into Pentwater.

Bicycle Sales, service

Gambles of Hart, State & East Main, Hart; (616) 873-2510.
The Bicycle Depot, 4462 Stanton Rd., Montague; (616) 893-BIKE.

Area attractions

Craig's Cruisers Fun Park, Mears; (616) 873-2511.
Mac Wood's Dune Rides, Mears; (616) 873-2817.
Sandy Korners ORV Rental, Mears; (616) 873-5048

Area festivals and events

June: Asparagus Festival, Hart/Shelby.
July: Arts & Crafts Fair, Pentwater; Fourth of July fireworks, Silver Lake.

Travel information

Hart/Silver Lake Chamber of Commerce; (616) 873-2247.
Silver Lake Tourist Association; (616) 873-5048.
Silver Lake State Park; (616) 833-3083.

15 Hart-Montague Trail

Some friends and I discovered the Hart-Montague Bicycle Trail, Michigan's first linear state park, a few years ago and it's been a special place to us ever since. Located in Oceana County, a land of tart cherries, apples, picture-postcard farms and beautiful waterways; this trail offers a sampling of what West Michigan is all about.

The rail trail begins at the John Gurney Park in Hart and then forms a ribbon-like trail south to Montague, passing along the way clusters of wildflowers, small-town train depots, and inviting ice cream stands. What makes the trail so special is the feeling you get when you're on it. The ambience of nature combined with a small-town escape, away from the city, is the best part of the adventure. I suspect it's what train passengers felt when the trail was part of the Chicago and West Michigan Railroad, a line that was built in 1872 to connect Pentwater to Grand Rapids.

The communities along the Hart-Montague have enhanced the trail with parks, parking areas and other amenities. The successful

HART
MONTAGUE

BICYCLE TRAIL STATE PARK

completion of the trail in 1990 has been a catalyst to the Rails-to-Trails movement to develop other proposed trails from abandoned rail lines throughout Michigan. In fact, the state has a special grant program for development of trails that link communities through the conversion of abandoned railroads.

The fully-paved asphalt trail, a little over 22 miles long, begins in Hart and travels along the former C&O Railroad that was abandoned in 1981. This rail bed is flat, yet passes through rolling terrain of beautiful hills and valleys. The best part, of course, is the absence of auto traffic and that makes for a relaxing ride. On parts of the trail, you can see so far off into the distance that houses appear little more than dots on the landscape.

This bike trail is a great tour for large groups of cyclists. I once rode the trail with more than 15 other cyclists of all ages, including toddlers and pre-teens. All of us met in Shelby, (mile 8 of the trail), and naturally broke off into groups according to our speed. Some went 10 miles, others went 44 miles, pedaling the entire point-to-point trail then backtracking. Non-cyclists in your group can drop you off at the beginning and then spend the afternoon in Hart or better yet the Montague/Whitehall area, while waiting for you to finish the ride.

Montague and Whitehall, twin cities at the southern trailhead and home to just over 5,000 people, are the largest communities along the trail. The towns, located on the White River and White Lake, which empty into Lake Michigan, feature a nautical atmosphere. Much of their seafaring history can be seen at the White

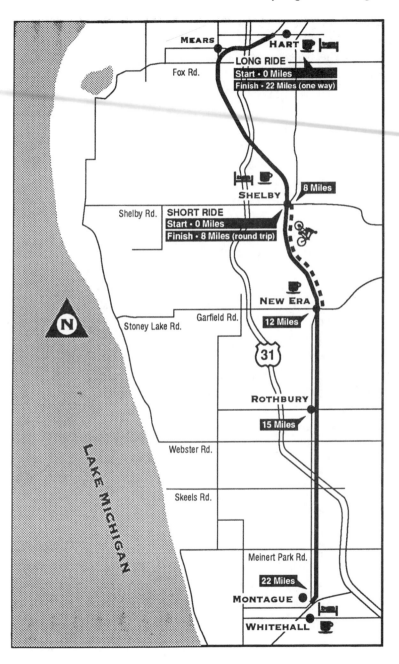

MEARS

HART

LONG RIDE
Start • 0 Miles
Finish • 22 Miles (one way)

Fox Rd.

SHELBY

8 Miles

Shelby Rd.

SHORT RIDE
Start • 0 Miles
Finish • 8 Miles (round trip)

NEW ERA

Garfield Rd.

12 Miles

Stoney Lake Rd.

31

ROTHBURY

15 Miles

Webster Rd.

Skeels Rd.

Meinert Park Rd.

22 Miles

MONTAGUE

WHITEHALL

N

LAKE MICHIGAN

127

River Light Station Museum (616-894-8265) built in 1875 over-looking Lake Michigan.

Hungry after your trail adventure? Try the Crosswinds Restaurant, just down the hill from downtown Whitehall, overlooking White Lake. It's a casual sit-down place, (accessible even by boat), and it's known for its fresh fish. There are also places to eat and small stores to stop for ice cream treats all along the trail. In Hart, the locals recommended the East Main Pub or the LaFiesta Mexican Food Restaurant as good dining spots.

A unique attraction in Shelby is the Shelby Man-Made Gem-stones (616-861-2165), which manufactures and sells man-made diamonds, rubies, sapphires and emeralds at a fraction of the cost of the real thing. There's a showroom with interpretive displays and an audio-visual theater that shows a program on the process.

Lodging and other bicycle services will improve as the trail continues to grow in popularity. But already there's Hart's John Gurney Park for those who want to combine camping and cycling. The modern campground has 104 sites on Hart Lake and is ideally located near the beginning of the trail.

For easy transport, there's Paul's Bike Trail Shuttle, which opened in 1994. They provide shuttle service at both ends of the trail to eliminate the problem of how to get back to your car. Brochures are available along the route or call (616) 773-2875 for rates, times and all services available.

Trail Fee The linear state park is also an excellent tune-up for the biking season, a good way to put in 44 miles, on a flat, fast surface. Being a state park there is, however, a user fee for cycling on the trail. The required trail passes can be purchased at various businesses along the trail, including Cherry Valley Hardware in Hart, the Country Variety Convenience Store in New Era and the Bicycle Depot in Montague. Or they can be obtained from park rangers who patrol the trail. The passes are available on a daily or annual basis for individuals or families. The trail passes are the major source of revenue for the upkeep of the trail.

Two cyclists pause In New Era along the Hart-Montague Bike Trail.

Stage one (8 miles) From the trailhead near John Gurney Park, head south on the asphalt trail to begin what many feel is most scenic of the two halves. The trail quickly passes through town and swings southwest, where in less than a mile, it crosses Polk Road, part of the Silver Lake route (page 117). You'll cycle under US-31 at 1.3 miles and then at 2.5 miles have the opportunity to depart the trail north for a short side trip into Mears. The small village is an interesting place (see page 123) that also features small shops and more great places to eat!

Back on the trail, just before Mile 3, you'll find the first of three picnic areas with tables located near the trail. From this "cycler's rest area", the trail winds its way eastward, crossing Baseline Road and Buchanan Road before you reach the town of Shelby at 8 miles.

In Shelby (population 1,624), the trail jogs behind Michigan Avenue, which is the town's business district. There are several places to eat nearby such as the Pizza Factory (616-861-5036), the Wooden Nickel Restaurant (616-861-5910) or the Fireplug Restaurant (616-861-2300), which serves Hudsonville ice cream. For those with a bike bag full of food, Getty Field is about a block from the trail and has a source of water while Memorial Park is two blocks from the former depot downtown.

Stage two (4 miles) From Shelby, the trail heads south, crossing Baker Road at 9 miles and then Grant Road. The only wooden trestle on the trail is located between Shelby and New Era. The small town of New Era is reached at mile 12 of the route and features a trailside park specially designed for Hart-Montaque Trail users. Here you'll find a very nice shelter, restrooms and a scenic bridge over a small stream. This is not only a very pleasant spot but you're also halfway to Montague. Time for an extended break.

Stage three (10 miles) From New Era, the trail makes a beeline to Montague, closely paralleling Oceana Drive almost the entire way. You cross Arthur Road at 13 miles and then Cleveland Road shortly after that. At Mile 15, you reach Rothbury, where you'll find a picnic area, restrooms, water and play equipment - in case your children are not already worn out from the ride. From Rothbury, it's a quick seven miles to the end of the trail in Montague. Along the way keep an eye out for bluebird boxes attached to trees. If you are lucky, you might spot an adult bluebird hunting insects, nest building or courting a mate.

At the southern trailhead, located near Old US-31 and Stanton

Boulevard in Montague, there is a special parking area for trail users, a small pavilion and restrooms. Located on the same corner is Trail End Miniature Golf and Ice Cream along with a convenience store, gas station and the Bicycle Depot for spare parts and repair.

Shorter option With plenty of parking areas near the trail, there are many shorter trail options. A nice 8-mile option is to start in Shelby and head south to New Era before doubling back.

Bicycle rentals, sales and service

Rothbury Hardware & Farm Supply, Rothbury; (616) 861-2418 or 894-8590.

Gambles of Hart, State & East Main Street, Hart; (616) 873-2510.

The Bicycle Depot, 4462 Stanton Blvd., Montague; (no phone).

Paul's Bike Trail Shuttle, (616) 773-2875.

Area attractions

Mac Wood's Dune Rides, Mears; (616) 873-2817.

Shelby Man Made Gems, Shelby; (616) 861-2165.

White River Light Station Museum; (616) 894-8265.

Area events and festivals

June: Asparagus Festival, Hart & Shelby; White Lake Area Arts & Crafts Festival, Whitehall.

August: White Lake Maritime Festival, Whitehall.

Travel information

Silver Lake State Park; (616) 873-3083.

White Lake Area Chamber of Commerce; (616) 893-4585.

Hart/Silver Lake Chamber of Commerce; (616) 873-2247.

Shelby Chamber of Commerce; (616) 861-4054.

New Era Chamber of Commerce; (616) 861-5219

Rothbury Chamber of Commerce; (616) 894-2385.

Heading to Lake Michigan on the edge of the Nordhouse Dunes.

16 Nordhouse Dunes

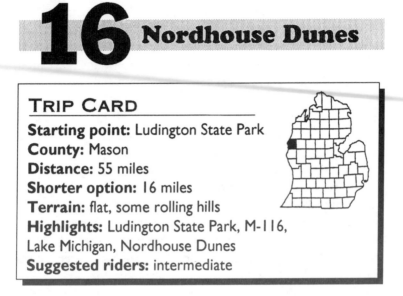

TRIP CARD

Starting point: Ludington State Park
County: Mason
Distance: 55 miles
Shorter option: 16 miles
Terrain: flat, some rolling hills
Highlights: Ludington State Park, M-116,
Lake Michigan, Nordhouse Dunes
Suggested riders: intermediate

M-116 is a friend to bicyclists. This road hugs the Lake Michigan shoreline and connects the town of Ludington to the Ludington State Park, the second largest state park in the Lower Peninsula. There are nicely paved shoulders on both sides of it with signs designating the road as a bike route.

This stretch on M-116 is definitely one highlight of a 55-mile cycling route encompassing Ludington and part of the Manistee National Forest, located south of Manistee. Lake breezes, wide open sand dunes, a fabulous state park, the town of Ludington, even a designated wilderness area makes this varied route enjoyable for cyclists. Beginners will find the flatness, spectacular scenery and length of the M-116 portion perfect as a shorter option route.

The 55-mile route begins at the state park and follows Lake Michigan, before heading north out of Ludington, on inland roads. Then almost as scenic as M-116, cyclists head west along the newly resurfaced Lake Michigan Road into the heart of the Manistee National Forest where it ends at the Lake Michigan Recreation

Area on the edge of the Nordhouse Dunes, a federally designated wilderness. This 6-mile road is a cool, shaded avenue that cyclists will appreciate on any hot, sunny day. The lush foliage, blue sky above, and occasional deer that peak out from behind the trees will refresh and energize you. At the end of the road in the recreation area, there is a beach, campground, picnic area and two wooden stairways where you can stretch your legs with a climb to the observation platforms overlooking the Lake Michigan shoreline. The second half of the trip is a return to the state park and includes backtracking on both Lake Michigan Road and M-116.

It's easy to see why the Ludington State Park campground is full almost daily from late June through Labor Day. This 5,200-acre park includes 4.4 miles of Great Lake shoreline, another 4 miles along Hamlin Lake and a series of spectacular dunes between them. There is also a short, paved bike route that follows Big Sable River, connecting to the park's Great Lakes Interpretive Center before merging onto M-116. If that wasn't enough physical activity for you, the park also features an 18-mile network of hiking trails, including a loop that winds through the dunes to the picturesque Big Point Sable Lighthouse.

Ludington is a year-round tourist destination but not the glamorous resort town that Saugatuck (some would say suburb of Chicago) is. Ludington is more a place for charter fishing, family-owned motels and cozy cottages on Hamlin Lake. There are a variety of shops and stores in downtown Ludington but our personal favorite, and that of most cyclists (or campers, runners, hikers, beachgoers...) is Ludington's House of Flavors (616-845-7360); it's the best place for rock-hard ice cream. There's nothing that hits the spot, or satisfies the sweet tooth more, than a hot fudge sundae after a long biking excursion on a warm, summer day.

A description of Ludington would not be complete without mentioning the Lake Michigan Carferry, with rooms for 520 passengers, 120 autos and unlimited bicycles on the 410-foot. S.S. Badger. This service to Manitowoc, Wisconsin, was reinstated in 1992 and is a four-hour (well, most of the time, weather permitting)

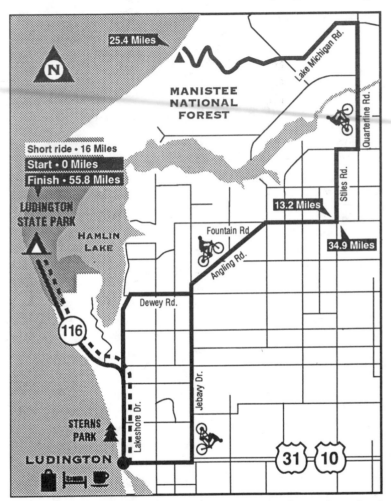

hassle-free cruise across the lake. Manitowoc is located north of Milwaukee and south of Door County, another popular destination for cyclists.

Stage one (8.2 miles) From the parking lot of the park's beachhouse (daily vehicle permit or annual pass required to enter the state park), head south on M-116, which is a flat road with wide shoulders and green and white bike route signs. Here the state's unique dune country will be on your left and Lake Michigan on the right. M-116 is literally an endless string of scenic spots along the Great Lake with access points from which to watch the sunset, listen to the waves or enjoy the sandy beach. The camper registration and information area is passed at 2.4 miles and at 3.8 miles you enter a wooded area briefly before taking a hard left to head north on Lakeshore Drive at 4.1 miles. This road has no shoulders, but is not heavily traveled. It twists and curves to follow Hamlin Lake for a stretch with the nicest views reached at 5.7 miles just before you pass Vacation Lane Resort.

The road curves to the right (east) and becomes Neal Street, passing more views of the lake and continuing to wind north until it turns into Stearns Road. The Sauble Resort (616-843-8497, housekeeping cottages) is passed at 6.2 miles and a quarter mile later you turn right (east) on Dewey Road; a narrow, tree-lined road with no shoulders. Turn left (north) on Jebavy Drive at 8.2 miles and Hamlin Grocery will be on the left and another market on the right. Time for a break, maybe??

Stage two (17.2 miles) From Jebavy Drive, immediately turn right on Angling Road at 8.4 miles to head northeast through rows of trees and open farm country. When the road curves sharply to the right at 10.9 miles and heads due east, you'll be on Fountain Road, which has shoulders on both sides. Turn left (north) on Stiles Road at 13.2 miles; pass more rolling fields until the road ends at Town Line Road at 15.4 miles. Turn right (east) and then left in a half mile to continue north along Quarterline Road by traveling up a slight hill. A "Welcome to Grant Township" sign will greet you at 16 miles followed by a long, gradual uphill segment at 17.6 miles.

Now for one of the best parts of the tour! Turn left (west) on Lake Michigan Road at 19.5 miles and follow this nicely resurfaced road as it twists, turns and winds its way through the Manistee National Forest. The road ends at the Lake Michigan Recreation Area at 24.6 miles. There's a campground to your left and the beach

Young cyclists on the bike path in Ludington State Park.

straight ahead, reached in less than a mile. Definitely get off those bicycles and enjoy a extended break with a walk along the wooden stairway over the dunes and down the shores of Lake Michigan.

Energetic bikers can climb one of two sets of stairways to observation platforms on the top dunes. One stairway is nearby and leads to the trailhead into the Nordhouse Dunes Wilderness Area. The other is in the picnic area (tables, shelter, water and play equipment). This stairway is a 160 steps up but provides the best vantage point of the Lake Michigan shoreline.

Stage three (23.8 miles) From Lake Michigan, backtrack the way you came, on Lake Michigan Road to Quarterline Road where at 31.4 miles you turn right (south). There's a couple of gradual uphills segments before you turn right (west) on Town Line

Road at 34.9 miles. You continue to retrace the route by turning left (south) on Stiles Road at 35.4 miles and right (west) on Fountain Road at 37.5 miles. There are some gently rolling hills on this road before Fountain curves to your right at 39.8 miles and becomes Angling Road.

On the return, however, you turn left on Jebavy Drive at 42.4 miles and follow it south through both open farm country and residential areas as you get closer to Ludington. After a long uphill stretch, you finally reach civilization at 47 miles when just ahead of you appears a McDonald's restaurant! Here you turn right (west) on M-116 which is also the west end of US-10. *Careful: even though this portion of the road is wide, it's the busiest in Ludington, especially during the summer.*

As you cycle toward downtown Ludington, you'll pass several motels and a couple of bed & breakfast in century-old Victorian homes. In the downtown area, there are several restaurants, such as Subway, A&W and Old Hamlin Restaurant. At 49.2 miles, you reach Lake Michigan again and can take a break at the Ludington City Park which overlooks a beautiful stretch of beach and provides facilities such as restrooms, a source of water and picnic tables.

Stage four (6.6 miles) From the City Park, head north on M-116 towards Ludington State Park. After a few blocks of sidewalks, you'll be on the designated bike route, with wide paved shoulders (yeah!). You'll cycle past the Cartier Park Campground and cross Lincoln River at 50.8 miles. A sign cautions you about sand drifting on the pavement but stay on course; the Lake Michigan scenery and cool breezes are definitely worth a little bit of blowing sand. This stretch is truly a cyclist's dream and before long you're back at the entrance to the state park at 55.8 miles.

Shorter option (16 miles) From the Hamlin Dam in the Ludington State Park, cycle out of the park on bike paths to M-116 and head south, closely hugging Lake Michigan. Pedal into Ludington to the City Park on Lake Michigan and then backtrack to the state park on M-116. This is a very popular bike outing for families staying at Ludington State Park.

Bicycle repair
Bicycle Circus, 404 S. James St., Ludington; (616) 845-1326.
Trailhead Bike Shop, 216 W. Ludington Ave., Ludington; (616) 845-0545.

Area attractions
Lake Michigan Carferry Service Inc., Ludington; (616) 843-4241 or (800) 845-5555 for taped information

White Pine Village and the Rose Hawley Museum, Ludington; (616) 843-4808 or (616) 843-2001.

The Train Station, Manistee; (616) 723-2889.

Area events and festivals
May: Carferry Festival, Ludington.

June: West Shore Art League Fine Arts Fair, Ludington.

July: Manistee National Forest Festival, Manistee; World of Arts & Crafts, Manistee.

August: Gold Coast Festival Arts & Crafts Fair, Ludington; West Michigan Fair, Ludington.

Travel information
Ludington Area Convention & Visitors Bureau; (800) 542-4600.

Ludington State Park; (616) 843-8671.

Manistee County Chamber of Commerce; (616) 723-2575.

Camping and biking can be easily combined at Mitchell State Park, the start of the Lake Cadillac Tour.

17 Lake Cadillac Loop

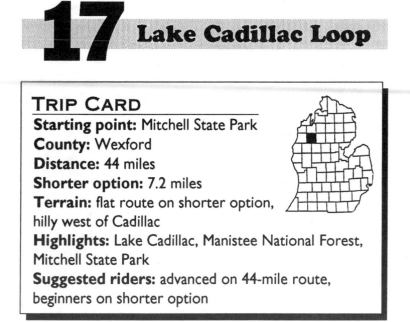

TRIP CARD

Starting point: Mitchell State Park
County: Wexford
Distance: 44 miles
Shorter option: 7.2 miles
Terrain: flat route on shorter option, hilly west of Cadillac
Highlights: Lake Cadillac, Manistee National Forest, Mitchell State Park
Suggested riders: advanced on 44-mile route, beginners on shorter option

Contrary to what some people believe, no Cadillacs roll off of any auto assembly lines in Cadillac! Many people associate Michigan with cars and automatically assume that Cadillacs are manufactured in Cadillac. Let me assure you; they are not.

What this city of 10,000 does have is two large inland lakes with a state park between them. Ninety miles north of Grand Rapids and near the Manistee National Forest, Cadillac has plenty of recreational activities to enjoy including hiking, camping and cycling.

Departing at William Mitchell State Park, between Lake Cadillac and Lake Mitchell, cyclists can ride around Lake Cadillac on paved bike paths that are ideal for beginners. This lakeshore circuit is a flat route with lakeshore scenery and three parks, including a mile-long park near downtown Cadillac and the Kenwood Nature Center. Downtown Cadillac is a fun place to lock up the bicycles and go on a shopping outing, take in a concert or be part of any of a number of events held annually.

For more experienced cyclists, the longer route heads north and then west into the Manistee National Forest. This loop, with some long hills heading back toward Cadillac, offers a challenging workout through some beautiful forests. The road south of tiny Harrietta winds and twists through the forest while M-55 East, sometimes a busy highway, is more wide open with nicely paved shoulders.

There are not many places for food on this longer route so it's best to bring along a high energy snack or picnic lunch and then plan on more serious eating back at your state park camp site or at one of the many restaurants in Cadillac.

In May, you can combine cycling with another favorite Cadillac and Mesick area activity - morel mushroom hunting. The Harrietta State Fish Hatchery, located west of Harrietta, offers another option for a family activity while at the state park is the new Carl Johnson Museum, the Michigan Hunting and Fishing Interpretive Center, just opened.

Stage one (7.2 miles) From the day-use beach area and parking lot to William Mitchell State Park, head south on M-115 which quickly merges into M-55. Here you'll find a paved a bike path on the left. In 0.7 mile, the road will curve left (east) past an "East M-55" sign. At this point, the designated bike route is on wide, paved shoulders that hug the lake. There are many residential homes along Lake Cadillac while South Shore Motel, a small establishment with 15 rooms, is on your left at 1.8 miles. The road curves sharply to the right at 3 miles (now called Granite Street), and takes you a through a residential section. At this point the bike path gives way to sidewalks. Cycle as close to the lake as possible and turn left on Laurel Street; take a right on Hector Street which merges into to Lake Street. Welcome to downtown Cadillac!

Downtown Cadillac offers an array of shopping and restaurants. The Sweet Shop (616-775-2201), on South Mitchell Street, is famous for its "Snowbird" candies. Made right on the premises,

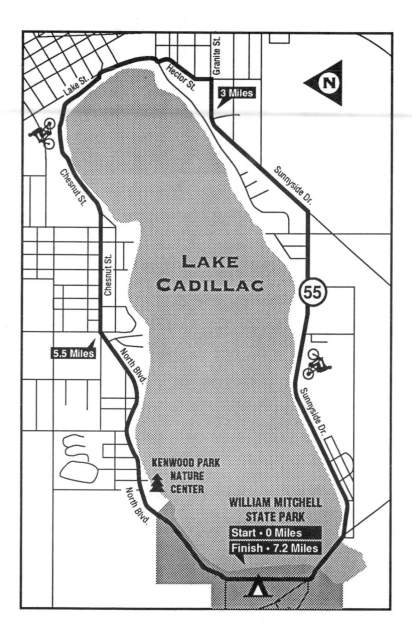

LAKE CADILLAC

WILLIAM MITCHELL STATE PARK
Start • 0 Miles
Finish • 7.2 Miles

KENWOOD PARK NATURE CENTER

3 Miles

5.5 Miles

it's an addicting treat of white chocolate and pecan pieces - a natural for cyclists. For more of a fine dining experience, visitors will enjoy Hermann's European Cafe and Chef's Deli (616-775-9563), located in a century-old building on North Mitchell Street. It's a place known for its European atmosphere and delicious desserts. There's also an inn at Hermann's with rooms and suites. Room rates include an extensive continental breakfast.

Access to Lake Cadillac and a nice picnic and playground area is at 4 miles where you'll also find restrooms and a source of drinking water. At this point, the bike paths return and you turn left on Lake Street at 4.2 miles and then take another left (west) on Chestnut Street, closely following the north shore of Lake Cadillac. You'll cycle by Cadillac Middle School at 4.7 miles and remain on Chestnut Street until you veer left onto North Boulevard at 5.5 miles. This road winds down to the lakeshore again, with paved shoulders on both sides, reaching it at 6.1 miles. This is the most pleasant section of the lakeshore route with views of Lake Cadillac and stands of hardwoods across the road. You'll cycle through a nice section of trees and then reach the Kenwood Park Nature Area. Operated by the city of Cadillac, the area includes a community beach, hiking trails, restrooms, a source of drinking water and public boat launch. The Carl Johnson Museum is also located nearby.

You'll find bike paths on the right at 6.5 miles and then cross Clam Lake Channel which connects Lake Mitchell and Lake Cadillac. The canal was dug in 1873 after loggers grew tired of floating timber from one lake to the sawmills on the other, through swampy Black River, a slow and laborious task not to mention the bugs they must have encountered. Today the channel is 48 ft. wide and used by recreational boaters, anglers and ducks looking for handouts from park visitors.

The campground at Mitchell State Park borders the south shore of the canal and at 7.3 miles you return to M-115.

Stage two (16 miles) Turn right (north) at M-115. This can be a busy highway, in fact at the end of holiday weekends this can

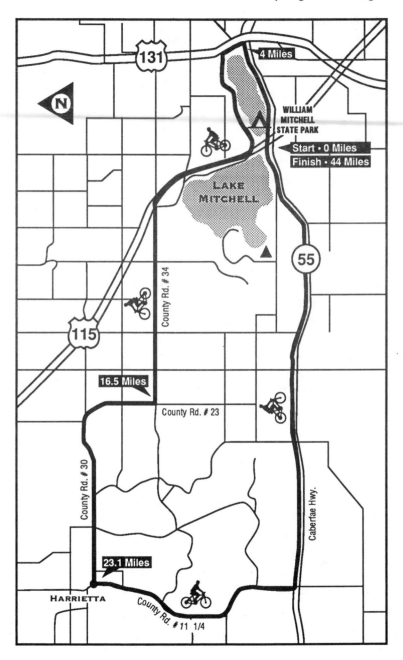

be the Indianapolis 500 with people rushing to get home. But it has nicely paved shoulders on both sides of the road and you only stay on M-115 for 3 miles. You'll quickly pass a Day's Inn at 7.5 miles and then enter open country with sprinklings of birch trees at 8.4 miles before turning left (west) onto County Road 34 at 10.6 miles. Along this narrow road with gravel shoulders you'll cycle through a pleasant stand of trees at 13 miles that give way to scads of wildflowers. There are some rolling hills on this section, beginning at 13.4 miles and eventually you re-enter a heavily wooded section of the Manistee National Forest.

More wide open country returns when you swing sharply right (north) at 16.5 miles and at one point you can see far off into the distance. You are now on South County Road 23 and after passing cornfields you enter the town of Boon. Well, "town" might be stretching it, as Boon consists of little more than a Christmas tree farm, railroad tracks, several mobile homes and a gas station. A post office is passed at 17.4 miles and then the route becomes more interesting as it runs parallel with the Ann Arbor Railroad tracks for 6 miles to Harrietta. Along the way you climb a hill at 18.1 miles, pass more farmlands bordered by wildflowers that contrast nicely with the wooded areas that follow. At 23.1 miles, you will come upon the sleepy town of Harrietta, where you'll find a small park and stately St. Edwards Catholic Church but few food options (bummer!).

Stage three (7.7 miles) From Harrietta, backtrack south on Davis Avenue, also called 13 1/2 Mile Road. This road twists and turns through more wooded areas in the Manistee National Forest and then winds over a number of hills as you make your way back to M-55. Most of them are easy-to-pedal, rolling hills but you tackle a long one at 28.5 miles. At one point the road swings right (west) and becomes County Road No. 11 1/4 Mile Road before curving back east as County Road No. 13 near Caberfae Ski Resort.

The third stage ends with a fun hill and a couple of big curves. At 30.8 miles you arrive at a parking area to the east. This is a nice time to get off your bicycles and munch down on the refreshments you've packed along (you did, didn't you?).

Stage four (13.2 miles) From the parking lot, head south on County Road No. 13 and within a quarter mile turn left (east) on M-55. This state highway can be busy, although you'll find narrow, paved shoulders here. More rolling hills are encountered along this stretch and probably the largest uphill pedal on this Cadillac route is tackled at 33.1 miles. After a few more hills, it's evident that civilization lies ahead as the number of homes and businesses increase. A Huron-Manistee National Forest ranger station and information facility is passed at 39.1 miles, where you'll find information and maps for hiking, canoeing and camping. At 42.9 miles you pass views of Lake Mitchell.

You'll cycle by Bill Oliver's Resort & Conference Center (motel, restaurant, golf course and bowling alley) and then enter the Cadillac city limits at 43.7 miles. It's now a short jaunt back to William Mitchell State Park, reached by turning left (north) on M-115. Time for a dip in the lake?

Shorter option (7.2 miles) From William Mitchell State Park, turn left (east) on M-55. The road curves sharply to your right and becomes Granite Street. Turn left (north) on Laurel Street and then turn right on Hector Street to end up on Lake Street into downtown Cadillac. The return begins by turning left (west) on Chestnut Street. Stay to the left at the intersection with North Boulevard and this road will take you back to the entrance of William Mitchell State Park.

Bicycle sales, service
McLain Cycle Shop, 311 N. Mitchell St., Cadillac; (616) 775-6161.
Area attractions
Johnny's Wild Game & Fish Park, Cadillac; (616) 775-3700.
Harrietta State Fish Hatchery, Harrietta.

Area events and festivals

May: Morel Mushroom Month, Mesick.

June: Lakefront Days, Cadillac.

July: Festival of the Arts, Cadillac; Fireworks over Lake Cadillac, Cadillac (July 4th).

Travel information

Cadillac Area Visitors Bureau; (800) 22-LAKES or (616) 775-9776.

18 Crystal Lake

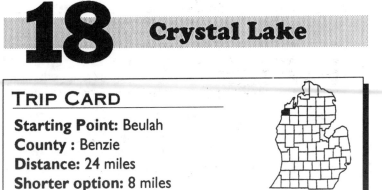

TRIP CARD

Starting Point: Beulah
County : Benzie
Distance: 24 miles
Shorter option: 8 miles
Terrain: flat, some hills at the end of the longer loop
Highlights: Beulah, Gwen Frostic's Studios,
Suggested riders: intermediate, beginners
for shorter loop

After cycling around Crystal Lake, it's easy to see why so many people make the area their second home. A stretch of the longer loop, on South Shore East and South Shore West, hugs the shoreline of Michigan's ninth largest lake and many feel one of the most beautiful. True to its name, Crystal Lake is an exceptionally clear body of water 8 miles long and set at the foot of rolling hills and sand dunes off of the Lake Michigan shoreline.

For much of this route you are either passing scenic views of the water or summer homes that have been traditional escapes for generations of the same family. Unlike most modern condominiums that look like boxes stacked on top of each other, these cottages each display their own distinct style and character. From three-story mansions with numerous bay windows, to simple one-story homes for weekend getaways, you'll marvel at the variety of homes along this stretch.

The one thing that most do have in common are bicycles; in the garages, gracing front lawns or parked out front along a roadway that is predominantly flat with nice, paved shoulders on both sides. Cyclists of all ages can usually be found riding most summer afternoons.

Located just south of the Sleeping Bear Dunes National Lakeshore, Crystal Lake is definitely worth a day of cycling. A convenient place to begin your 24-mile shoreline circuit is Beulah, a picturesque town in a valley at the east end of the lake. Beulah is a great place to explore and enjoy a variety of eateries, and, of course, the shops and boutiques that flourish in many northern Michigan towns. The Cherry County Cycling Club recommends Northern Delights Bakery and Deli in Benzonia and pizza and beer at the Hungry Tummy in Beulah. There's also a variety of lodging, from the luxurious Brookside Inn in Beulah (616-882-7271 or 616-882-9688), which offers rooms with Polynesian spas, to RV campgrounds, full service resorts and Chimney Corners (616-352-7522), your quintessential northwoods inn. We parked at the Cherry Hut (616-882-4431), a place for good food like their homemade cherry pie (with locally grown cherries) and great cinnamon bread.

From Beulah, the longer loop heads south into Benzonia, a slightly smaller town, then heads west along rustic River Road to another unique attraction, Gwen Frostic's Studios (616-882-5505). Frostic is a noted poet, publisher, artist and conservationist, who has lived in the area since the 1960's. Here she has created a personal wildlife sanctuary of 285 acres and a small publishing company where workers print block designs carved by her onto cards, stationery, wall prints and books.

If you travel clockwise around Crystal Lake, there are a few hills and some turns in the beginning, then the route flattens out for the rest of the journey. The loop circles the lake at its west end on M-22, passing through Pilgrim, a tiny community near the Point Betsie Lighthouse on Lake Michigan. This popular lighthouse is every photographer and artist's dream at sundown on a clear evening.

For beginning cyclists, the shorter option begins in Beulah and goes counterclockwise, to avoid the immediate and somewhat

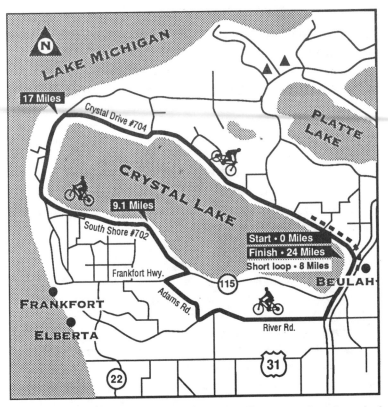

intimidating hill coming out of Beulah into Benzonia. One friend of mine, returning to cycling after a long absence from the sport, easily handled four miles around the lake on the shorter route before heading back to enjoy a leisurely afternoon in Beulah.

Another way to add distance to the 24-mile loop is to cycle back to where you are staying. We stayed at the Platte River Campground, a marvelous facility operated by the Sleeping Bear Dunes National Lakeshore. Cycling from this campground would add another 14 miles to the circuit around Crystal Lake. Recently renovated at a cost of more than $4 million, the National Park Service campground features pull-through modern sites along with rustic sites and even more secluded walk-in sites, especially designed for cyclists. Kids will have a fun time just cycling the campground's newly paved roads. The facility makes a fantastic home base when cycling in the Crystal Lake area or touring the popular Sleeping Bear National Lakeshore area.

By accident, we found a terrific spot, near the campground, where Lake Michigan Drive deadends. This is where the Platte River empties into Lake Michigan and families can spend an afternoon lazily floating down the river on tire tubes into the "big" lake. For a long float on the Platte there is Riverside Canoes (616-325-5622) at the corner of M-22 and Lake Michigan Road, where you can rent canoes, kayaks, tubes, rafts and paddleboards. Riverside Canoes also has a full-service general store with groceries, camping supplies and souvenirs. This is the perfect place to pick up a well-deserved Dove Bar after a bike ride or stock up on firewood for an evening campfire.

Stage one (3.4 miles) From Beulah head south on US-31. After a heart-pounding effort uphill, turn right (west) on River Road (also called Traverse Avenue), which is fairly narrow and has gravel shoulders. Within 3.4 miles you reach Gwen Frostic Prints.

Her location on River Road is the ideal atmosphere for her artistic endeavors. The large galleries are housed in a building of native stone, glass and old wood where inside you'll find rough-cut beams, stone fireplaces and natural fountains. You'll be surrounded by Frostic's poetry books, woodblock prints and wildlife carvings by noted artists. Even more impressive is the publishing aspect of the gallery. From a balcony above, you can view 15 original Heidelberg presses clanking away as workers print a wide selection of cards, notepaper and wall prints. The gallery is open daily May through November and Monday through Saturday the rest of the year.

Stage two (9.1 miles) From Gwen Frostic's head right (west) on River Road and in 5.3 miles you will cross the Betsie River at 5.3 miles. Turn right on Adams Road, a narrow road with no shoulders to quickly cross the Betsie River a second time. You're now in the Betsie River State Game Area; the rustic, even

Printers working on the presses at Gwen Frostic's Studio.

"wilderness-like" scenery makes for interesting cycling.

You turn left (west) on Casey at 6.9 miles and then jog to the right (east) on M-115 at 7.1 miles where you encounter a long downhill segment. It ends with a panoramic view of Crystal Lake to the north just before you turn left (north) on Shorewood Drive at 7.6 miles. After climbing a long hill, the road twists and curves and climbs a few more times before you turn right (east) on Lobb at 9.1 miles. This road curves to left and becomes South Shore East (also Country Road 702), well named as it hugs the Crystal Lake shoreline. Eventually it changes to South Shore West, a flat road with paved shoulders on both sides that winds past a variety of cottages and the sandy shoreline of the lake.

Stage three (11.5 miles) From South Shore West, turn right on M-22, which is also called Pilgrim Highway. Soon you'll pass Point Betsie Road, where you can detour for a short side trip to the lighthouse. The lighthouse is not open to the public but towers above a sandy beach in a very scenic stretch of Lake Michigan shoreline.

M-22 has wide shoulders as well as bike route signs along this stretch and beyond mile 17 of the tour winds past Chimney Corners. At one time a downhill ski area, today Chimney Corners is a lakeside resort with 25 housekeeping cottages and one of the best restaurants in the county. Dinner is served only in single seatings Monday through Wednesday and double seatings Thursday through Saturday in a 1910 lodge made with hand-stripped logs and filled with antiques.

At the corner of M-22 and Crystal Drive, turn right (east) on Crystal Drive. This road, lined by cottages, is flat with paved shoulders, making it ideal for beginners. Crystal Drive follows the lakeshore until merges into US-31. From here it's a short jaunt back to the starting point in Beulah. Time to enjoy a cherry dessert at the Cherry Hut.

Shorter option (8 miles) From Beulah, head counterclockwise by pedalling north on US-31 to Crystal Drive and then turn left (west). Follow this flat road as far as you want, but within four miles you come to a nice spot to view the lake and rest a spell before backtracking to Beulah.

Bicycle rental

Sleeping Bear Trekking Co. & Clothiers, 6516 Western Ave., Glen Arbor; (616) 334-6228.

Sugar Loaf Resort, 4500 Sugar Loaf Mountain Rd., Cedar; (800) 748-0117.

Bicycle sales, service

Weiler Cycle Works, 180 S. Benzie Blvd., Beulah; (616)882-9253.

Area attractions

Gwen Frostic Prints; (616) 882-5505.

Riverside Canoe Trips; (616) 325-5622.

Area events and festivals

July: Fourth of July festivities, Frankfort and Beulah; Beulah Art Fair, Beulah.

August: Blueberry Festival, The Maples in Frankfort; Frankfort Art Fair; National Coho Festival, Honor.

Travel information

Benzie County Chamber of Commerce; (616) 882-5802.

Traverse City Area Convention & Visitors Bureau; (800) TRAVERS or (616) 947-1120

Cherry Capital Cycling Club, P.O. Box 1807, Traverse City, MI 49685-1807 (Send $6 for a waterproof, foldout map which features other suggested cycling routes in northwest Michigan.)

Running down the famed Dune Climb in Sleeping Bear Dunes National Lakeshore.

19 Sleeping Bear Tour

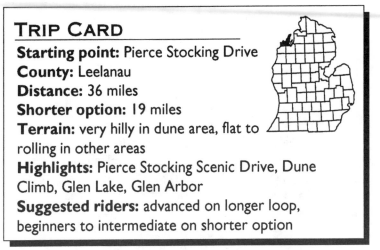

TRIP CARD

Starting point: Pierce Stocking Drive
County: Leelanau
Distance: 36 miles
Shorter option: 19 miles
Terrain: very hilly in dune area, flat to rolling in other areas
Highlights: Pierce Stocking Scenic Drive, Dune Climb, Glen Lake, Glen Arbor
Suggested riders: advanced on longer loop, beginners to intermediate on shorter option

Obviously cyclists were not left out when the National Park Service rehabilitated the 7.4-mile long Pierce Stocking Scenic Drive in the 1980s. How refreshing it is to see a wide, paved shoulder and a sign that says "Right Lane for Bicycles Only," after entering the road in the Sleeping Bear Dunes National Lakeshore.

This scenic drive is definitely the highlight of a 36-mile route that winds through the national lakeshore and around Glen Lake. The drive was named after Pierce Stocking, who spent his youth working as a lumberman in the area and later came up with the idea of a road to the top of the dunes so people could enjoy the incredible scenery from high above Lake Michigan. The road first opened to the public in 1967 and was called Sleeping Bear Dunes Park. After Stocking's death in 1976, the road was renamed in his honor. The loop is challenging because of the many long uphill climbs and exciting descents that follow. Cyclists must use the right side of the road and the route is recommended for experienced riders only. However, beginners can still enjoy driving through the dune area and then cycling the 19-mile shorter loop around the Glen Lakes.

Almost as scenic as Pierce Stocking Drive is Glen Lake, well-known for its sparkling blue waters. The lake has a unique shape, something of a warped hourglass. In the middle is the "narrows" where a bridge crosses between the two sections of the lake. The smaller half to the west is only 12-feet deep while the main part is 130-feet deep in places, although cyclists don't have to worry about that.

Another highlight of the route is Glen Arbor, a picturesque town with a variety of lodging choices from bed & breakfast establishments and family resorts to the luxurious Homestead Resort (616-334-5000). There are also several unique shops such as the Totem Shop (616-334-3533) for Petoskey stones or Indian souvenirs, and Wildflowers (616-334-3232) for beautiful table centerpieces, perennials and wildflowers.

Stage one (7.4 miles) This is the Pierce Stocking Scenic Drive portion of the route. At the beginning of the drive there is a parking area to leave the vehicle followed by a contact station where you can pick up an interpretive brochure that corresponds to numbered posts. Along with scenic overlooks, Pierce Stocking Scenic Drive includes a series of well-marked stops where you can learn about dune ecology and other natural topics. You are then faced with an immediate uphill segment, a good indication of the hills to come. There are shoulders on both sides of the road and soon you'll see a sign that says the right lane is for bicycles only (how nice!). Within the first mile you have a long downhill stretch that bottoms out at a covered bridge and a pull-over nearby so you can take time to enjoy the scenic spot.

More steep ascents and descents are followed by a scenic overview of Glen Lake at 1.9 miles and then Picnic Mountain. The day-use area is reached at 2.2 miles and includes tables, water,

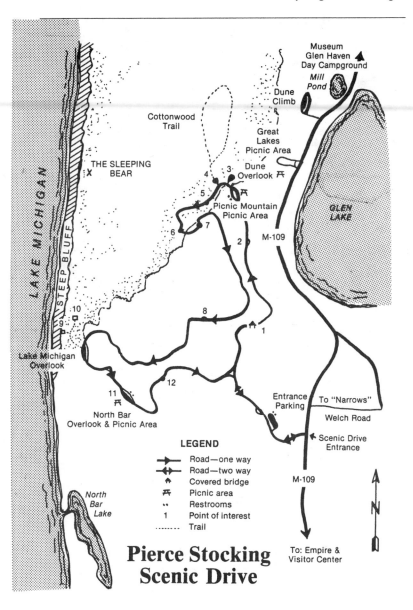

Pierce Stocking Scenic Drive

LEGEND

Road—one way
Road—two way
Covered bridge
Picnic area
Restrooms
Point of interest
Trail

The covered bridge along Pierce Stocking Scenic Drive.

restrooms and access to Dune Overlook, the first of three spectacular viewing points of the surrounding dune country and Lake Michigan. All three overlooks have bike racks and the first two have short trails into the dunes. The trail at Dunes Overlook is Cottonwood, a 1.5-mile loop with an interpretive brochure available from a box at the trailhead.

Another tedious hill is encountered at 2.7 miles and is followed by a couple of sharp curves and hills, more hills, and even more hills! At 5.5 miles you reach the Lake Michigan Overlook where from 450 feet above Lake Michigan you have an excellent view of its shoreline and all the way to Platte Bay, 9 miles to the south, if the visibility is good. North Bar Overlook and Picnic Area with tables and restrooms is a short ride away, and from there Pierce Stocking Scenic Drive winds its way back to the entrance.

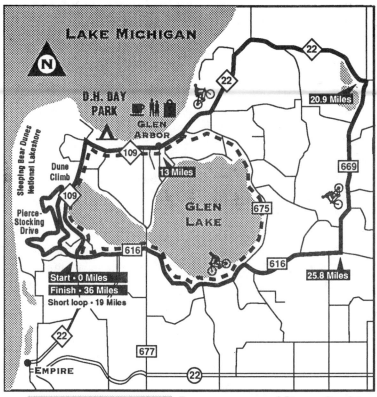

Stage two (6.1 miles) From entrance of Pierce Stocking Scenic Drive, turn left on M-109, a road with paved shoulders on both sides. You can see Glen Lake on the right and Lake Michigan sand dunes to your left at 8.2 miles and in a half mile will arrive at three National Park Service day-use areas, one almost immediately following the other. The first is a picnic area at the base of a dune on the left side of M-109, and the second on the same side of the road is the Dune Climb. This is, without question, the most popular stop in the Sleeping Bear Dunes as thousands of visitors annually make the steep climb up the wind-blown, 130-feet high dune. It's a slow trek up on foot, but the view on top is spectacular and the run back down wild. You'll also find restrooms here, a few tables, drinking water and a small store open during the summer. The Dune Climb is also a good alternate starting point for your ride, as it will keep non-cyclists happy while they wait for you. A little further north along M-109 at 9.9 miles is the Glen Lake Beach with picnic tables, water and a small sandy beach.

At 10.9 miles, just south of Glen Haven, M-109 turns sharply to the right (east). Continuing straight ahead is M-209 which makes an interesting detour. By following it you would quickly pass through the ghost town of Glen Haven and end up at the Sleeping Bear Point Maritime Museum, where the National Park Service has preserved a U.S. Life Saving Station that was built in 1901.

This tour, meanwhile, follows M-109 to the east and immediately passes the entrance to D.H. Day Campground at 11.5 miles. The 88-site, National Park Service campground is a rustic facility and a very popular one that doesn't reserve sites in advance. It also provides access to one of the most beautiful beaches in Michigan. Cycle to the log cabin shelter in the back of the campground where you will find a short foot path to Lake Michigan. Here the sand is sugar white, the water a shade of turquoise and the scenery stunning, with the Manitou islands on the distant horizon.

Continuing east on M-109, you enter Glen Arbor, 2 miles from the campground or Mile 13 of the tour. Within this quaint town there's the Glen Arbor Bed & Breakfast and Cottages on your left and the Totem Shop, a unique gift shop on your right. There's also a mini-mart, restaurants and gas station, (need air in your tires?) on the left at 13.5 miles. If baking on the beach isn't your idea of the perfect extended break, then Glen Arbor is a nice alternative where you can walk around, do a little souvenir shopping or get a bite to eat.

Stage three (15 miles) M-109 ends in Glen Arbor and you continue north on M-22 to quickly pass The Homestead Resort at 15 miles. Billing itself as America's Freshwater Resort, The Homestead has two restaurants, condominiums that are rented out year round, its own private beach and complete ski facilities (both downhill and Nordic). It also has prices to reflect all this. On this longer loop, you continue north then east of Glen Lake on M-22

The dune terrain seen in Sleeping Bear Dunes National Lakeshore.

as the road winds through rolling hills, and past picturesque farms. At 20.2 miles, you pass Bass Lake and then at 20.9 miles turn right (south) on County Road 669. This road is narrow, no shoulders, yet lightly travelled; you pedal past School Lake on the right within a half mile. There's no public access on the lake but you get a glimpse of the water here and there through the shoreline trees.

You move into rolling farm country and at 25.8 miles, turn right (west) on County Road 616, another narrow road with no shoulders. You'll cycle through a residential section and then at 28.2 miles CR-616 begins winding its way towards Burdickville.

Stage four (7.5 miles) Keep cycling on CR-616, which in Burdickville merges briefly with County Road 675. The Glen Lake Inn (fine food, cocktails) is on your right at 29 miles. CR-675 heads south, but the tour stays on CR-616 which winds along the south side of Glen Lake. At 34 miles you arrive at the "narrows", where

M-22 cuts the lake in half. You'll find hand-dipped ice cream at The Narrows Motel & Dairy Bar (616-334-4141), where rooms and double dips makes for a profitable combination. From the "narrows", it's only 2.4 miles back to the starting point. Where CR-616 curves sharply to the right (north), keep cycling straight ahead on Welch Road to quickly return to the entrance of Pierce Stocking Scenic Drive.

Congratulations, you've completed a strenuous loop, made easier by the knowledge that you're in one of Michigan's most beloved areas. Time to meet up with your non-cycling family members who are at the Sleeping Bear Dune Climb or relaxing in camp.

Shorter option (19 miles) Convenient starting points for this shorter option around Glen Lake are the entrance to Pierce Stocking Scenic Drive, Glen Arbor or the Glen Lake picnic area on M-109. From the entrance of Pierce Stocking Scenic Drive, turn left (north) on M-109. Keep cycling on M-109 after it makes a sharp right and heads east into Glen Arbor. Head north out of town on M-22 then turn right (east) on County Road 675. This road winds around Glen Lake and merges into County Road 616 at Burdickville. Stay on CR-616 as it passes the "narrows" and where it curves sharply to the right (north), keep cycling straight ahead on Welch Road to return to the entrance of Pierce Stocking Scenic Drive.

Bicycle renting

Sleeping Bear Trekking Co. & Clothiers, 6516 Western Ave., Glen Arbor; (616) 334-6228

Sugar Loaf Resort, 4500 Sugar Loaf Mountain Rd., Cedar; (800) 748-0117 or (616) 228-5461.

Area attractions

Sleeping Bear Dune Climb, M-109, Sleeping Bear Dunes National Lakeshore.

Sleeping Bear Point Maritime Museum, M-209, Sleeping Bear Dunes National Lakeshore.

Returning from the Lake Michigan beach in D.H. Day Campground.

National Park Service Visitor Center (displays, audio visual presentation, information), Empire.

Travel information

National Park Service; (616) 326-5134.

Traverse City Area Convention & Visitor's Bureau; (800) TRAVERSE or (616) 947-1120.

Cherry Capital Cycling Club, P.O. Box 1807, Traverse City, MI, 49685-1807 (send $6 for foldout waterproof map with other suggested cycling routes for northwest Michigan.)

20 Lake Leelanau

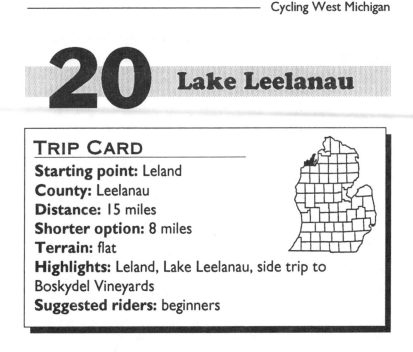

TRIP CARD

Starting point: Leland
County: Leelanau
Distance: 15 miles
Shorter option: 8 miles
Terrain: flat
Highlights: Leland, Lake Leelanau, side trip to Boskydel Vineyards
Suggested riders: beginners

Beginning cyclists seeking a short, flat route in the otherwise hilly northwest Michigan, won't have to look any further than the upper portion of Lake Leelanau. This delightful journey, beginning in Leland, offers a sampling of what the region is best known for; fruit markets, public beaches and Leland, one of northern Michigan's most delightful lakeside communities.

The most charming aspect of Leland is its nautical atmosphere. The village's trademark is a row of weathered dockside shacks along the Leland River that at one time housed commercial fishermen and today is a historical district known as "Fishtown." The commercial fishermen are gone but their buildings have been preserved and now house gift shops and restaurants, including The Bluebird, (616-256-9081) an eating establishment that's been around since 1927 and specializes in fresh fish and mesquite-broiled seafood. Adding to the maritime setting is the fact that the ferries to both North and South Manitou depart from the docks of Fishtown.

More shops and restaurants are found on Main Street in Leland, including the Early Bird restaurant, which has excellent food and is a favorite destination for Cherry Capital Cycling Club members.

An ideal two-day get-away would be to combine a cycle tour of Lake Leelanau with a day trip to South Manitou Island, a part of Sleeping Bear Dunes National Lakeshore. You can get to this beautiful retreat via the Manitou Island Transit (616-256-9061), which offers daily trips throughout the summer. Once on the island visitors can enjoy an island tour, hike the trails and old farm roads, view a shipwreck (from land no less!) or climb 116 steps to the top of a lighthouse.

Still want more riding time after 15 miles of cycling? The roads around the lower part of Lake Leelanau make for an interesting 46-mile loop. The tour is not only longer but harder as you encounter many hills. Attractions on the lower portion of the lake include Monstrey's General Store (616-946-0018), a place for handmade wooden toys and bike repair, and the tasting room of the Boskydel Vineyard (616-256-7272), one of the most beautiful wineries in the state.

Stage one (4 miles) From the heart of Leland, cycle north on M-22 to quickly escape the Izod-clad tourists strolling downtown. This portion of M-22 has gravel shoulders and within the first mile you climb one of the few hills along the loop. There are nice views of Lake Leelanau at 2.1 miles and then at 3.2 miles you turn right (south) on County Road 641. The road closely follows the lake as it twists and turns its way south to Lake Leelanau. At 4 miles, just after crossing Houdek Creek, you pass a lake access site. The facility also includes a picnic area overlooking the lake and a parking area, which could easily be used as an alternative starting point for your trip.

Stage two (5.5 miles) From the picnic area, continue south on CR-641 as it follows the shoreline of Lake Leelanau. The road is flat here as it passes views of the water, winds through stands of

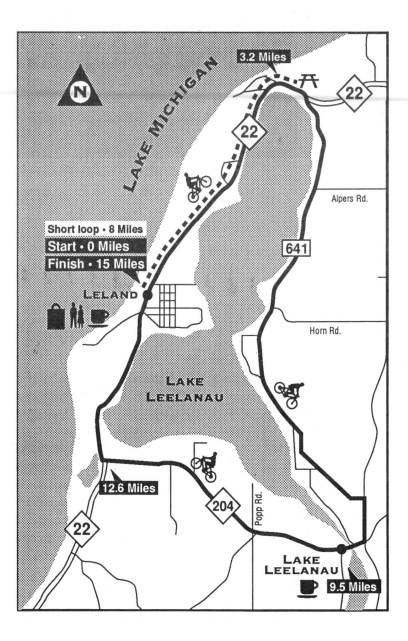

birch trees or young orchards on the surrounding hills. The county road swings more to a southeast direction near Warden's Point and you take a sharp curve to the left at 6.8 miles and another sharp left a mile later.

After a downhill segment passing more views of the lake and orchards, CR-641 makes a 90-degree turn to right (south) where Eagle Highway merges into it. At 9.1 miles you come to a stop sign at the intersection of CR-641 and M-204, where an arrow points toward the town of Lake Leelanau. Turn right (west) on M-204. The Leelanau County Chamber of Commerce is passed on the right at 9.5 miles in Lake Leelanau, a scenic and untouristy (unlike Leland) town that straddles the two halves of its namesake lake.

For a delightful side trip, and to add another 7 miles to this route, cycle south from the town of Lake Leelanau on County Road 641 to Boskydel Vineyard on Otto Road. Boskydel is the first bonded wine cellar on the peninsula and from its small parking lot you have a view of sloping vineyards leading down the hill right to the edge of Lake Leelanau. The surrounding scenery once prompted a Chicago Tribune wine critic to call Boskydel the most beautiful winery in the Midwest. The wine isn't bad either and in this tasting room they plop down a large wine glass, not some one-ounce plastic cup. The winery is open year-round from 1-6 p.m.

Stage three (5.5 miles) M-204 is a wide road with nice, paved shoulders on both sides and is relatively flat. Occasionally during the summer you'll encounter heavy traffic on it. From Lake Leelanau, the road veers northwest until it ends at the junction with M-22 at 12.6 miles. Turn right (north) on M-22 and within a third of a mile the state highway will begin to wind along the edge of the lake. This portion of M-22 can also have a lot of traffic on it but is flat with wide shoulders on both sides of the road.

Two miles south of Leland you'll pass The Manitou Market & Bakery (616-256-9156), an excellent fruit market with fresh baked goods, a deli, local wines, maple syrup, homemade jams and jellies as well as healthy stuff like fruits and vegetables. After 14 miles,

A cyclist takes a break at an abandoned barn in Leelanau County.

you'll cycle into the heart of Leland and pass the dam in town. Try not to run over any fudgies.

Shorter option (8 miles) Cycle north out of Leland on M-22 and turn right (south) on County Road 641 to a picnic area and lake access. The access site is reached within four miles and makes a nice place for lunch before backtracking to Leland.

Bicycle sales, service

City Bike Shop, 322 S. Union, Traverse City; (616) 947-1312.

Ralston Cycle, 750 E. Eighth, Traverse City; (616) 941-7161.

Great North Sports, 104 E. Front St., Traverse City; (616) 946-3290.

Brick Wheels, 430 W. 14th St., Traverse City; (616) 947-4274.

McLain Cycle, 2786 Garfield Rd. S, Traverse City; (616) 941-8855.

Monstrey's General Store & Sport Shop, 8332 E. Bingham Rd., Traverse City; (616) 946-0018.

Bicycle rental

Laughing Fish, Fishtown, Leland; (616) 256-8878.

Sugar Loaf Resort, 4500 Sugar Loaf Mountain Rd., Cedar; (800) 748-0117 or (616) 228-5461.

Area events and festivals

July: Leland Wine & Food Festival, Leland; National Cherry Festival, Traverse City; Leland Art on the Lawn, Leland.

August: Suttons Bay Art Festival, Suttons Bay; Leelanau Peninsula Wine Festival.

September: Leelanau Harvest Bike Tour.

October: October Festival, Northport; Fall Festival, Suttons Bay.

Travel information

Traverse City Area Convention & Visitors Bureau; (800) TRAVERS, or (616) 947-1120.

Cherry Capital Cycling Club, P.O. Box 1807, Traverse City, MI 49685-1807; (send $6 for foldout, waterproof map with other suggested cycling routes for northwest Michigan.)

21 Old Mission Tour

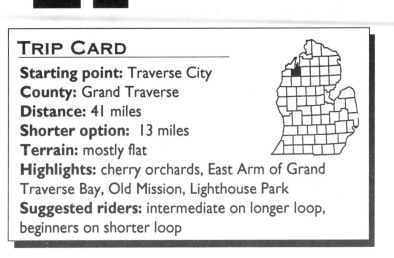

TRIP CARD

Starting point: Traverse City
County: Grand Traverse
Distance: 41 miles
Shorter option: 13 miles
Terrain: mostly flat
Highlights: cherry orchards, East Arm of Grand Traverse Bay, Old Mission, Lighthouse Park
Suggested riders: intermediate on longer loop, beginners on shorter loop

Grand Traverse Bay. It's not so much a place as a feeling of being "up north" that lures people back to the area time and time again. The county is known for its waterways - inland lakes, bays, rivers and, of course, Lake Michigan. But it is the bay itself, with the Traverse City skyline on the south end, and split in the middle by historical Old Mission Peninsula, that is the crowning jewel of the region.

There is no better way to enjoy the bay, its scenic shoreline or the area's famous cherry harvest than by this 41-mile bike journey. You will traverse Old Mission Peninsula through one of highest density of cherry trees in the world; ripe, red, shiny cherries ready for eating if biking this route in July. Stunning blossoms will greet you in mid-May. You will travel a road that winds its way by the East Arm of the bay and then loops back along the West Arm, where across the water are the rolling hills of Leelanau Peninsula.

Vineyards, fruit markets, a restaurant with an outdoor patio, a tavern in historic Old Mission and finally a classic lighthouse in a pleasant park are all a part of the tour. Old Mission Peninsula is 18 miles long, while at its narrowest point this finger of land is less than a mile wide. This route is primarily flat, with a few hills thrown in to justify a hardy lunch. A beautiful stretch of the route is Bluff Road, which closely hugs the shore of the East Arm. There's no shortage of food choices on the peninsula. Area cyclists recommend Kelly's Roadhouse (616-223-7200) and Old Mission Tavern (616-223-7280) for homemade soup, great sandwiches, a wonderful selection of beer and walls that double as an art gallery.

This Old Mission Peninsula route is an excellent escape for anybody staying in Traverse City. Serving as the hub to northwest Michigan, Traverse City offers a plethora of lodging and lots of eateries. There are also a wide range of attractions and activities including para-sailing, sailing cruises, elaborate miniature golf courses, shopping, hot air balloon rides, orchard tours and a museum of automated musical instruments. Plenty of pre-ride and post-ride options for everyone in your group.

Stage one (13.6 miles) Begin at Bryant Park, a small city park on the southwest end of the Old Mission Peninsula, just off M-37/US-31 in Traverse City. Turn left (north) on M-37 and right (east) on Eastern Avenue at 1.3 miles. Traverse City High School will be on your right and makes for another good starting point. Here you will find a separate bike path on the right. Turn left (north) on Birchwood (also called East Shore Road), a road with unpaved shoulders but beautiful views of the East Bay. At 4.4 miles, Birchwood (East Shore Road) deadends into M-37 where you turn right to continue north. M-37, which ends at the northern tip of the peninsula, has wide, paved shoulders at this point, which is good because it can be a busy road at times, especially on the weekends in the summer and during autumn colors (early October).

At 5.4 miles, you begin a slow but steady climb with a beautiful view of the bay to the right. Keep an eye out for Bluff Road where you turn right to depart M-37. Bluff Road is an exceptionally scenic

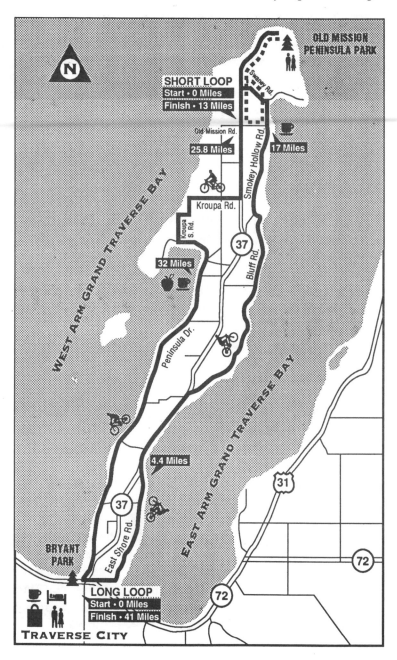

section of the route that closely hugs the shoreline offering panoramic views of the water and the other side of the East Arm. At 13.6 miles, the road makes a sharp left before you turn right onto Smokey Hollow Road.

Stage two (7.6 miles) Cycle north on Smokey Hollow Road where at 14.5 miles you'll encounter a long, steep climb past cherry orchards. A climb up another large hill ends with a gorgeous view of the placid bay below. Smokey Hollow ends at Old Mission Road at 17 miles where you turn right.

You've reached the historic Old Mission at 17.3 miles. Old Mission was settled in 1839 when Rev. Peter Dougherty arrived from Mackinaw City and established a Presbyterian missionary; 12 years later a post office was established. Postmaster Stone received no pay and it is said that he kept the mail in an empty box nailed to his kitchen wall. When the letters arrived at Elk Rapids across the bay, smoke signals were sent up and somebody would paddle a canoe over to pick it up.

When the mission moved to the west side of the bay in 1852, Stone also took over the trading activities with local Indian tribes and built a store. Today, that store is Lardie's General Store, which for 82 years was managed by three generations of the Lardie family. Inside you'll find shelves and coolers stocked with refreshments or you can just take a break on the rambling wooden porch. Just down the street is a replica of the Old Mission Church that provides a better historical insight into the store and the area.

At 17.7 miles, just past Old Mission Inn & Campground, turn left (west) on Swaney Road. At 18.6 miles, turn right (north) back on M-37 (also called Center Road) and you'll reach the entrance to the Lighthouse Park at 20.4 miles. The Old Mission Lighthouse is almost another mile along the road. Built in 1870, the tower and adjoining lightkeeper's house sits just south of the 45th Parallel, the halfway point between the Equator and the North Pole. You'll find interpretive displays on this and the history of the lighthouse along with a beautiful beach, picnic tables, restrooms and hiking trails.

The lighthouse at Lighthouse Park on the tip of Old Mission.

Stage three (8.8 miles) After your break at the lighthouse, it's time to start the journey back. Head south on M-37 to pass a nice view of the West Arm at 22.1 miles. Cross back over Swaney Road at 23.8 miles to start a long uphill stretch. You pass the junction to Old Mission Road at 24.9 miles and then struggle up another long hill, reaching Old Mission Tavern (616-223-7280) at 25.8 miles. If a beer is not your pleasure at this point you'll pass several sweet cherries stands that are usually selling fruit from early July to mid-August.

Turn right on Kroupa Road at 26.9 miles. This road is hilly, with no shoulders and curves sharply to your left (south) where on many maps it becomes Kroupa Road South although it wasn't actually marked in the real world. In the next 3 miles you encounter a sharp curve in each direction and then a gentle hill before turning left (east) onto Ne-ah-ta-wanta Road at 30 miles. Here you'll find an arrow pointing to Bowers Harbor.

Stage four (11.5 miles) Ne-ah-ta-wanta Road twists and curves to the south as it skirts Bowers Harbor, passing a public access site to the bay at 31.2 miles. Turn right at the stop sign by the Harbor Station to quickly reach Bowers Harbor Inn (616-223-4222). The restaurant is renown throughout northwest Michigan for its fine cuisine and steep prices. It's a little upscale for most cyclists in spandex.

The road continues to hug the West Arm for the rest of the route and becomes Peninsula Drive at 39.7 miles, where you will undoubtedly notice the wide shoulders on both sides. You're back in Traverse City at 40.8 miles and shortly after that Peninsula Drive merges into M-37. The state highway will curve to the right and at 41.5 miles you will be back at Bryant Park. It's time to rest, sample those cherries you bought or head further into the downtown area to lounge on the sandy beaches of the Grand Traverse Bay.

Shorter option (13 miles) Begin on the northern portion of the Old Mission Peninsula. Cycle counter clockwise, beginning at Old Mission Tavern. Take Old Mission Road to Smokey Hollow Road then turn left (north) to Lardie's General Store in Old Mission village. Turn left (west) on Swaney Road and then make an immediate right (north) on M-37 which leads to the Lighthouse Park. From the lighthouse, backtrack south on M-37 to the starting point at the tavern.

Bicycle sales, service
City Bike Shop, 322 S. Union, Traverse City; (616) 947-1312.

Ralston Cycle, 750 E. Eighth, Traverse City; (616) 941-7161.

Great North Sports, 104 E. Front St., Traverse City; (616) 946-3290.

Brick Wheels, 430 W. 14th St., Traverse City; (616) 947-4274.

McLain Cycle, 2786 Garfield Rd. S, Traverse City; (616) 941-8855.

Monstrey's General Store & Sport Shop, 8332 E. Bingham Rd.; Traverse City; (616) 946-0018.

Area attractions
Amon Orchards; (616) 938-9160.

Clinch Park Zoo; (616) 922-4903 or (616) 922-4905.

Grand Traverse Balloons; (616) 947-RIDE.

Music House; (616) 938-9300.

River Country Funland; (616) 946-6663.

Tall Ship Malabar; (616) 941-2000.

Traverse Bay Para-Sail; (616) 947-2628.

Underwood Orchards & Country Store; (616) 947-8799 or (616) 947-8764.

Area events and festivals

June: Old Mission Art Fair, Traverse City.

July: National Cherry Festival, Traverse City.

August: Downtown Traverse City Art Fair.

Travel information

Traverse City Area Convention & Visitors Bureau: (800) TRAVERS or (616) 947-1120.

Traverse City Area Chamber of Commerce; (616) 947-5075.

Cherry Capital Cycling Club, P.O. Box 1807, Traverse City, MI 49685-1807 (send $6 for foldout waterproof map with suggested cycling routes for northwest Michigan.)

Trilliums are found throughout the northern Michigan woods.

 **22 Beethoven Amble**

┌───┐
TRIP CARD

Starting point: Interlochen
County: Grand Traverse, Benzie
Distance: 34 miles
Shorter option: 12 miles
Terrain: flat on shorter loop, rolling
to medium hills on the longer loop
Highlights: Interlochen State Park, Interlochen
Center for the Arts, Green Lake, Long Lake
Suggested riders: beginners on the shorter loop,
intermediate on the longer route
└───┘

    Imagine camping in a state park with sounds of a string quartet, a jazz ensemble, classical music or a little Bach floating through the air...followed by the sounds of applause ringing through Michigan's north woods. These are all possibilities when visiting Interlochen State Park, located next to the world-renowned Interlochen Center for the Arts.

    Situated on a 1,200-acre campus, the Interlochen Center for the Arts is the umbrella organization for the Interlochen Arts Academy, the Interlochen Arts Camp and Interlochen Public Radio. The center is 16 miles southwest of Traverse City and over the years has built a reputation as an innovative center for teaching students music, theater, dance and the visual arts through a distinguished faculty and guest artists. More than 450 annual events take place in this culturally rich environment, including performances by the Oak Ridge Boys, Victor Borge, Linda Rondstadt, the

Manhattan String Quartet and Peter, Paul and Mary, among other famous entertainers. Visitors are free to sit in on classroom lessons and rehearsals, and campus tours provide a historical perspective of the center and its 450 buildings.

Practically next door is Michigan's second oldest state park. Interlochen was established in 1917 to preserve a small tract of virgin white pine that was passed over by loggers and lumber barons in the 19th century. Today, the park encompasses 187 acres of land between Duck and Green lakes and includes a mile of shoreline, 576 campsites and a day-use area on Duck Lake with a wide sandy beach, picnic tables and a shelter.

Both the virgin pines and the famous music camp are highlights of a 34-mile bicycle route that begins at the state park and circles Green Lake. It then heads northwest to the small town of Lake Ann, before looping back to the Interlochen via the west side of Long Lake. The 12-mile shorter option is a mostly flat route that circles Green Lake. Both rides traverse a beautiful forested area of hardwoods and pines, including one exceptionally scenic tract just inside Benzie County seen when you cycle across the Betsie River. It's one of those spots you would miss when in a car, one of those quiet surprises that are especially rewarding to cyclists. On a perfect Sunday afternoon in September I was awestruck at the simplicity of the gently flowing river, the cottony, white clouds against an azure sky, and the leaves just starting to show their colors.

A great natural area, but what about food and shopping on this route? Local cyclists recommend Boone's Long Lake Inn on East Long Lake Drive for a "feast to remember". Near the state park, on the corner of 31 and M-137, there's a strip of shops including Grandma's Kitchen which features homemade soup. There's also a bookstore and the Traverse Bay Woolen Company that offers items like wool sweaters and blankets, ski socks and winter jackets - a good place to do some early Christmas shopping! The Pipigwa Pottery & Gallery, 4 miles south of the Interlochen Center for the Arts, displays Odawa Indian pots, stoneware pottery and artwork

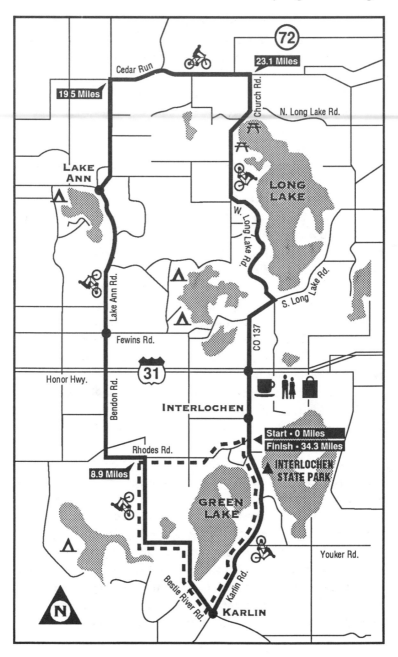

of several northern Michigan artists. Finally, Dove Song is a flower and gift shop on M-137 with a unique selection of baskets, souvenirs and other locally produced items.

Stage one (5.4 miles) Keep in mind that Interlochen State Park, any state park for that matter, requires a small vehicle fee or annual pass to enter it. From the parking lot in the park's day-use area on Duck Lake, cycle to the main entrance and turn left (south) on M-137. This road has wide, paved shoulders and winds through beautiful hardwoods and graceful, towering white pines. Green Lake Campground, the delightful rustic portion of Interlochen State Park, is passed at 0.4 miles and then in another mile M-137 curves to the west and becomes Karlin Road. More curves follow along with a gradual uphill stretch at 2.9 miles, where you will encounter gravel shoulders.

Eventually the road curves right into the small village of Karlin. Just before Karlin's blinking light at 4.1 miles you turn right on Betsie River Road and head northwest back towards Green Lake. The road curves immediately to the right through a stand of conifers followed by a large tract of mature hardwoods. After a few more twists and curves in the pavement, you reach a nice view of Green Lake at 5.1 miles and an even nicer spot overlooking the Betsie River at 5.4 miles. It's a great spot to pull your bicycle off the road and take a break, munch on a granola bar and feel the sun on your back.

Stage two (11.2 miles) From the scenic overlook, cycle north and stay on Betsie River Road as it makes a 90-degree turn to the left (west) and one to the right (north) at 6.8 miles. Turn left (west) on Rhodes Road at 8.9 miles (also called County Road 665) to pass through more stands of hardwoods and pines. Eventually the road curves sharply right (north) at 9.9 miles and becomes a rather bumpy Lake Ann Road. You pass through a residential area at 10.3 miles and immediately follow up a steep hill. Cross US-31 at 11.9 miles, but be careful! These motorized tourists are in a

The logger's "Big Wheel" on display at Interlochen State Park.

hurry! At this point, the route moves into open farm country where you will see a traditional white farmhouse with a stone foundation and the classic, faded red barn at 12.5 miles.

The hilly portion of the ride is now encountered. Take a deep breath and begin pumping, especially at 14.7 miles where you'll encounter a long uphill stretch. Birch Glen Resort is passed to your left at 15.8 miles followed by more hills before you reach the Lake Ann village limits at 16.3 miles. This is another beautiful part of the route as shimmering Lake Ann is to your left while the road curves sharply to your right at 16.6 miles. You'll find a couple of restaurants here (and thus restrooms).

Stage three (17.7 miles) Turn right in the village of Lake Ann on Lake Ann Road and immediately climb a steep hill. You make a couple of curves to the left and head out of town at 17 miles along a road that is also labeled County Road 665. This is primarily a flat portion of the route until you make a sharp curve to the right (east) at 19.5 miles and merge into Cedar Run Road. You encounter rolling hills and more stands of pine as the road curves sharply left (north) and then immediately right at 20.5 miles before continuing east. Turn right (south) on Church Road at 23.1 miles which ends at the northern tip of Long Lake. Here you turn right (to the west) on North Long Lake Road, a tree-lined avenue that hugs the shoreline of the lake.

Gilbert Park is reached at 24.9 miles and is a perfect place to enjoy a picnic, or to just stretch out on the grass. You'll find picnic tables, volleyball courts and a source of drinking water. There is also parking here, making the park a good alternate starting point for this route. More rolling hills are encountered as you head south on West Long Lake Road which eventually swings away from the lakeshore into a mixture of open farm country and hardwood trees.

The road makes a sharp 90-degree curve at 26.4 miles as it heads back towards the water and within a mile it winds to a nice view of Long Lake. You pedal through a shady tunnel of trees as West Long Lake Road continues to wind along the lake before ending at South Long Lake Road at 29.7 miles. Turn right (west) on South Long Lake Road (nice paved shoulders on this stretch) and in a half mile you'll be curving south heading for the intersection with US-31 and M-137 at 32 miles.

The intersection is a major one and is lined with businesses, including a grocery store, bookstore and restaurants. Just a quarter mile south on M-137 is the Interlochen Motel, where the room rate in the summer includes continental breakfast. Shortly, you will enter the village of Interlochen and more food options at Cicero's Pizza and the Pinepointe Grocery Store. The main entrance to the Interlochen Center for the Arts campus is reached at 34 miles while immediately to your left is the entrance to the Interlochen State Park. At 34.3 miles, you'll be back in the parking lot - your starting point. Have any energy left? Within the state park is Pines Nature

Trail, a mile-long loop that winds through towering white pine.

Shorter option (12 miles) From the day-use parking lot of Interlochen State Park, cycle to the entrance and turn left (south) on M-137, which becomes Karlin Road. Turn right on Betsie River Road, which curves sharply to your left and then to your right as it heads north. Turn right (east) on Rhodes Road and journey to M-137. Head south on M-137 to return to the state park.

Bicycle sales, service
Broken Spoke, 9661 Inwood, Interlochen; (616) 275-6843.
City Bike Shop, 322 S. Union, Traverse City; (616) 947-1312.
Ralston Cycle, 750 E. Eighth, Traverse City; (616) 941-7161.
Great North Sports, 104 E. Front.; Traverse City; (616) 946-3290.
Brick Wheels, 430 W. 14th St., Traverse City; (616)947-4274.
McLain Cycle, 2786 Garfield, Traverse City; (616) 941-8855.
Monstrey's General Store & Sport Shop, 8332 E. Bingham Rd., Traverse City; (616) 946-0018.

Area attractions
Interlochen Center for the Arts, Interlochen; (616) 276-9221.
Great Lakes Paleontological Museum, Long Lake; (616) 943-8850.
Pipigwa Pottery & Gallery, Karlin; (616) 263-7141.
Platte River Hatchery (4 miles west of Interlochen).

Area events and festivals
June: Interlochen Arts Festival, Interlochen through August)
July: Interlochen Art Fair, Interlochen Center for the Arts; National Cherry Festival, Traverse City.

Travel information
Interlochen State Park, Interlochen; (616) 276-9511.
Traverse City Area Convention & Visitors Bureau; (616) 947-1120 or 1-800-TRAVERS.
Cherry Capital Cycling Club, P.O. Box 1807, Traverse City, MI 49685-1807.

Petoskey stone hunters look for the state stone along the Lake Michigan shoreline.

23 Trip Around Torch

TRIP CARD

Starting point: Eastport
Counties: Antrim and Kalkaska
Distance: 47 miles
Shorter option: 4 to 8 miles
Terrain: mostly flat, some rolling hills
Highlights: Barnes County Park, Grand Traverse
 Bay, Torch Lake, Alden, fruit markets
Suggested riders: intermediate

When you look down while wading on the shores of Torch Lake, you see something unusual compared with many lakes further south; your feet! The water is crystal clear, allowing you to see any Petoskey stone lying on the lake's rocky bottom. Shaped like a torch, Torch Lake is 20 miles long, 2 miles wide and part of a chain of lakes that includes Elk Lake, Lake Bellaire and Intermediate Lake. But Torch is the crowning jewel of not only this chain but of northwest Michigan, a region, some would say, that is soaked with lakes, streams and shoreline. It's little wonder National Geographic once named this Antrim County body of water as one of the most beautiful lakes in the world!

Torch Lake is the highlight of this 47-mile route but so is Antrim County. The county is sandwiched between Grand Traverse County to the south and Charlevoix to the north and doesn't receive the travel writers' fanfare of either. What's missing here is the motel strips of Traverse City and the tourist-packed shopping areas of Petoskey. What you will find in Antrim County are small towns with historic main streets, acres of succulent cherry orchards and almost a never ending view of water.

This cycling trip around Torch Lake is an ideal way to see the countryside of Antrim County for those staying in a resort, campground or nearby motel. About half-way along the circuit, you pass through a town most people have never heard of, much less been to. Alden is a must stop for cyclists. It has small shops, an excellent restaurant and a historical depot being renovated into a local museum all in a hillside downtown area that slopes gently to the shores of Torch Lake. I was immediately impressed by this picturesque town with its unpretentious air. It's a nice place to stretch your legs with a stroll by the lake or grab a bite to eat. Try the hamburgers at the Alden Bar & Grill, breakfast at the Country Kitchen (616-331-6777), the breakfast buffet at the Torch Riviera (616-322-4100) or creamy ice cream at Scheiler's Soda Fountain and Ice Cream Parlour where they change the flavors daily.

Another well-kept secret is Barnes County Park, an Antrim County Park near Eastport at the northwest tip of Torch Lake. Although there's no fishing, boating facilities or hiking trails, the park has a pleasant campground and one of the most beautiful beaches around. This secluded beach on the Grand Traverse Bay has sugar-like sand that is bordered by towering pines, birches and other hardwoods.

Search the surf long enough and you might a Petoskey stone, Michigan's state stone. A Petoskey stone is actually fossilized corral, recognized by its distinctive honeycomb pattern. When dry, the stones are hard to distinguish from many other rocks on the beach. But when wet the pattern is hard to miss. That's why you will see people standing in the surf and holding handfuls of rocks just under the surface of the lake. If that's too much work for you, any decent gift shop will have polished Petoskeys for sale.

This tour begins and ends at Barnes County Park. There is no fee to use the beach or the picnic facilities at this 120-acre park but there is a fee to camp here. Barnes has 60 sites, half modern and

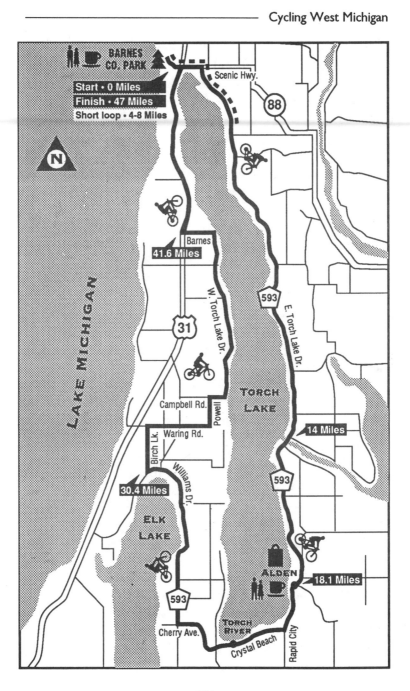

half rustic, with water, modern restrooms and showers. No reservations are accepted and in July through August the campground is usually filled on the weekends. Rarely is there a problem obtaining a site Sunday through Wednesday.

Stage one (11.6 miles) Starting from Barnes County Park, cycle clockwise around Torch Lake by first heading east on M-88. Cross the busy intersection at US-31 at 0.6 miles and immediately to the right you'll pass a public access site to the lake. Turn right on East Torch Lake Drive (also County Road 593) at 1.1 miles. The road immediately begins winding along the shoreline of Torch Lake as you head south. This road is not wide, but the traffic is normally light and the views of the water are excellent.

You enter a stand of hardwoods at 1.9 miles, followed by an open view of the lake and then encounter some rolling hills. If you need a break, browse through a flea market that is passed at 4.2 miles (you never know what kind of bargains you might find!). The route continues to wind south along the lake, passing through a heavily wooded area at 8.1 miles followed by a stretch of open farmland at 11.2 miles. Turn right (west) at the stop sign where there is an arrow pointing toward Alden at 11.6 miles. You'll still be on East Torch Lake, although it's now called East Torch Lake Road.

Stage two (7 miles) At 14 miles you enter the tiny hamlet of Clam River, where there are food possibilities, including Campbell's On Torch. Campbell's is a sprawling log cabin along 160 feet of prime Torch Lake frontage that serves everything from hamburgers and pizza to antipasto salad and baby-back ribs. You'll cross Clam River and then immediately cycle by Thayer Lake at 14.8 miles. Cedar Shores Resort is passed at 15.4 miles and a half mile later there is another good view of Torch Lake.

You'll enjoy a long downhill stretch at 17.1 miles and then the road curves to the right. At 17.8 miles East Torch Lake Road curves to the right and becomes Alden Highway. This will take you into

Cairn Monument, an interesting side trip on the Torch Lake tour.

the town after a sharp right hand (west) curve at 18.1 miles. You reach the downtown area at 18.6 miles and will find a variety of shops, an ice cream parlor, an old fashioned general store and Spencer Creek Landing, an excellent restaurant in a century-old Victorian house. It's pretty fancy (and expensive) but the couple that run it also have a low-key cafe next door where spandex cycling shorts fit in better.

Stage three (16.5 miles) Cycle south out of Alden. There's an uphill stretch at 19.2 miles where the road curves to the left and within a mile you'll be near the south end of Torch Lake. At this point the road has paved shoulders on both sides and you turn right (west) on Crystal Beach Road (still CR-593) at 20.4 miles. The south end of the lake is the border between Antrim and Kalkaska counties and you're actually pedalling in Kalkaska County. CR-593 curves to the left at 20.7 miles past views of the lake and then you cycle through Torch River. There is a small grocery store here and the Torch River Inn.

The road curves to the right at 23 miles and becomes Cherry Avenue (still CR-593) which begins with a long hill. More hills are encountered after you curve left at 23.9 miles and pass through the heart of Antrim County's cherry country. Cherry Avenue swings right to head due north at 26.7 miles and now features paved shoulders on both sides. You pass more cherry orchards, several large barns and even a glimpse of Elk Lake now and then. Eventually you swing to the left (west) and at 28.9 miles enter the sleepy village of Kewadin. You'll find a convenience store, the Oasis Bar and Grill and a few other small businesses.

Turn right (north) on Birch Lake Road at 30.4 miles. This road has gravel shoulders and is bumpy but has less traffic on it than Cairn Highway. Turn right on Winters Road at 31.6 miles and head east toward Torch Lake where it becomes Waring Road. You'll cross Cairn Highway (watch for traffic) at 32.7 miles, followed by a nice view to the east of orchards and then at 34 miles the road curves to the left (north) and becomes Powell Road. After climbing a long hill and then descending its backside, you turn right on Campbell Road, a narrow road with no shoulders, at 34.7 miles. A couple more hills and you reach Torch Lake at 35 miles where you turn left (north) on West Torch Lake Drive; just up the road is a public access site to the lake.

You can take a well deserved break here or make a slight detour to visit one of Michigan's most unusual monuments. Instead of crossing Cairn Highway, head north on it and within a mile you'll come to the Cairn Monument. Dedicated in 1938, the monument honors Hugh Gray, who was instrumental in promoting Michigan tourism. It features a stone from every county of the state and sits on the 45th Parallel, the halfway point between the Equator and the North Pole. There's no tables or restrooms here but it's a scenic spot; from the top of a hill you're surrounded by cherry trees while on the horizon is a view of Lake Michigan. To return to the route, backtrack to Campbell Road and turn left (east) to West Torch Lake Drive.

Stage four (12.5 miles) Cycle north on West Torch Lake Drive for some of the best views of the lake along the route. You'll pass through a stand of large pine at 38.6 miles that gives way to more views of this beautiful lake. You take on a short but steep hill at 41 miles and then the road curves sharply left (west) and on maps it becomes Barnes Road, although it wasn't marked. Turn right on US-31 at 41.6 miles for a 5-mile stretch up the busy road. Unfortunately the road has narrow shoulders on both sides so you must be careful!

Travel through the Village of Torch Lake where at 44.5 miles you pass Schoolhouse Antiques, an antique store located in a refurbished one-room schoolhouse. Torch Lake Township Day Park is passed next and then the Torch Crest Party Store is on your left at 44.6 miles. But hold off on food! Turn left at Barnes Lake Park Road at 47 miles and there will be an ice cream store on the right. Go ahead and get the triple dip; you're only about a half mile from where you began in Barnes County Park. When cycling or driving into the park, watch out for the large speed bumps!

If you're looking for something more substantial than ice cream, right at the corner of US-31 and M-88 is Molly Malone's, an Irish pub and restaurant with an excellent corn beef and cabbage boil dinner, Guiness beer on tap and, of course, Irish music at night.

Shorter option (4-8 miles) Cycle out of Barnes County Park and head east on M-88 and go clockwise around Torch Lake by heading east on M-88. Cross US-31 and then turn right on East Torch Lake Drive (also County Road 593). This road winds along the shoreline and is a scenic stretch. Pedal as far as you want to before turning around and backtracking to Barnes County Park.

Bicycle sales, service
Brick Wheels, 430 West 14th, Traverse City; (616) 947-4295.

City Bike Shop, 322 S. Union, Traverse City; (616) 947-1312.

Great North Sports, 104 E. Front St., Traverse City; (616) 946-3290.

McLain Bike Shop, 2786 S. Garfield, Traverse City; (616) 941-8855.

High Gear, 1103 Old Tannery Creek, Petoskey; (616) 347-6118.

Bicycle repair

American Cycle, 100 N. Division Rd., Petoskey; (616) 347-6877.

Area events and festivals

June: Art Fair, Elk Rapids.

July: R.A.T. (Ride Around Torch), Cherry Capital Cycling Club, Torch Lake; Venetian Festival, Charlevoix.

August: Harbor Days Festival (with bike races), Elk Rapids.

October: Apple Festival, Charlevoix.

Travel information

Traverse City Area Convention & Visitors Bureau; (800) 872-TRAVERS or (616) 947-1120.

Elk Rapids Chamber of Commerce; (616) 264-8202.

Cherry Capital Cycling Club, P.O. Box 1807, Traverse City, MI 49685-1807.

24 Hemingway Tour

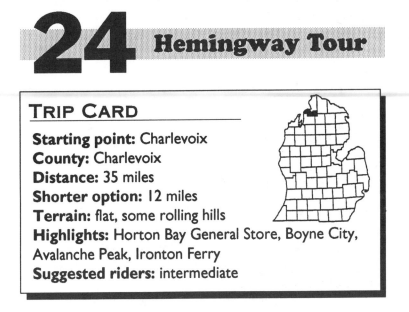

TRIP CARD

Starting point: Charlevoix
County: Charlevoix
Distance: 35 miles
Shorter option: 12 miles
Terrain: flat, some rolling hills
Highlights: Horton Bay General Store, Boyne City, Avalanche Peak, Ironton Ferry
Suggested riders: intermediate

Horton Bay, the town, was only five houses on the main road between Boyne City and Charlevoix. There was the general store and post office with a high false front and maybe a wagon hitched out in front...

Ernest Hemingway from "*Up in Michigan*"

Charlevoix. Ah, beautiful Charlevoix. Even its name is inviting. Charlevoix is a picturesque town, with multi-colored petunias lining the streets. As you approach, all eyes are drawn to a canvas of sailboats on tiny Round Lake, seemingly in the middle of the downtown area.

But Round Lake is just a teaser to the larger Lake Charlevoix, which makes an excellent 35-mile bicycling circuit if you bypass the south arm via the Ironton Ferry. Charlevoix, a town of more than 3,000 residents (it probably triples during the summer), is a good place to begin and end your bike ride. There are plenty of post-ride options such as shopping, art galleries and festivals throughout the vacation season. Non-cyclists in the group will be more than happy to wait here for the adventurous souls to complete their loop.

Pleasing terrain, wonderful scenery, many pleasant parks and a little bit of Hemingway history is what this challenging 35-mile circuit offers. Several of Ernest Hemingway's Nick Adams stories take place in settings from the area around Charlevoix and Walloon lakes while a description of Horton Bay General Store opens up his tale, "Up In Michigan." This two-story structure built in 1876 has a wide front porch, inviting visitors in to walk across its worn, wooden floors or idle away a summer afternoon as a young Hemingway often did. Inside is something of a shrine to its famous patron, with guns, old traps, mounted deer heads and numerous photos of Hemingway. It's still a general store, though, with ice cream, cold drinks and counter where the morning coffee drinkers gather.

The 49 residents of tiny Horton Bay don't seem to take themselves too seriously. Every Fourth of July the village hosts a wacky, tongue-in-cheek parade, which draws thousands of spectators. One recent parade featured Murphy Brown impersonators, the "Dan Quayle Spelling School" float, rock bands (instead of marching bands) on flatbed trailers, a parade viewing stand at the Horton Bay General Store, and llamas instead of horses.

A fun stopover on this journey around Lake Charlevoix is Ironton. To avoid cycling an additional 16 miles around the south arm of the lake, cyclists (and cars) can take passage on the Ironton Ferry for a five-minute ride across the arm. The historical ferry is beloved by the locals as it is no more than a barge on a cable and was once featured in the "Ripley's Believe It or Not" column. The ferry service dates back to 1876, and is operated on demand as operators can easily see when their service is needed. As a cyclist, it's fun to cruise ahead of the cars and not wait on a busy summer day as there's only room for four vehicles. But there is always room for another person on a bicycle.

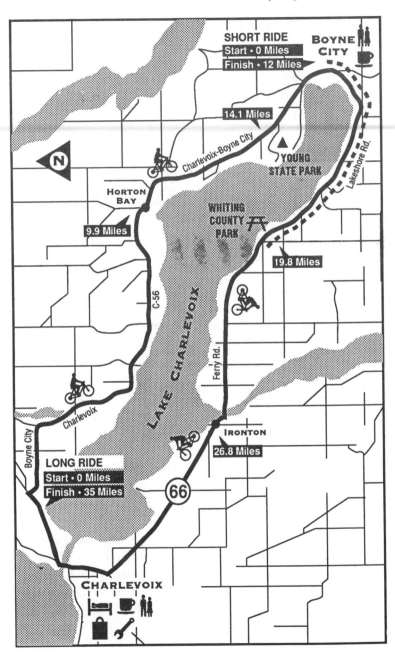

The south shore of Lake Charlevoix is definitely easier and flatter. A shorter option for beginners is to cycle from Boyne City on the south shore of the lake as far as desired and then backtrack to Boyne City. From Boyne City to the Ironton Ferry is just over 11 miles, a pleasant journey that closely follows the lake.

In Charlevoix, you'll find a wide variety of lodging and eateries. There are moderate-priced motels, luxurious condominium suites and six bed & breakfast establishments, including the Charlevoix Country Inn (616-547-5134) that was built in 1896 and overlooks Lake Michigan. For campers, there is Fisherman's Island State Park, 5 miles south of Charlevoix on US-31. The 2,678-acre park not only has some great beaches and good hunting for Petoskey stones but most popular are its 15 rustic sites right on the shoreline where your tent is only a few feet from the lapping waters of Lake Michigan.

To wind down after a workout, bicyclists can treat themselves to a customized cruise on the Voyageur, Cruises Unlimited (616-547-0188), or by taking a scenic cruise on the Miss Charlevoix (616-547-2371) or the Bay Breeze Schooner Co. (616-547-0024). And on your spare day you might consider a day trip to Beaver Island, known as the "Emerald Isle" for its strong Irish heritage. An unspoiled paradise, the island is a haven for mountain bikers with plenty of gravel roads. Beaver Island has a lodge, hotels and camp sites available along with a couple of interesting museums, specialty shops and lighthouses. The Beaver Island Boat Company (616-547-2311) offers passenger and car ferry service to the island. Every day from mid-June through Labor day, visitors can leave for the island in the morning and return to Charlevoix that same day.

Stage one (10 miles) We started this route from the VFW Hall, located north of the business district of Charlevoix, although any place in Charlevoix will work as a good starting point. Cycle the route in a clockwise direction, heading north out of Charlevoix. From US-31, turn right on Boyne City Road at 0.5 miles. This road has gravel shoulders and is hilly in places but lightly travelled. You

Hemingway's Horton Bay General Store, a popular stop along the Lake Charlevoix bicycle tour.

encounter a long hill at 1.6 miles and then the road winds it way south passing good views of Lake Charlevoix at 6 miles. More twists and curves follow and at 8.6 miles you head downhill past a llama farm.

A "Welcome to Bay Township" sign can be seen at 9 miles and another hill is confronted before you enter Horton Bay, population; 49! Horton Bay General Store will be to the left at 9.9 miles while nearby is the Red Fox Inn Tourist Room and Heartwell & Co. Bookstore. Horton Bay is a good place to get off those bicycles and have a look around where Hemingway used to hang out. The author not only idled away several youthful summers on the front porch of the old general store but also fished Horton Creek for brook trout and eventually celebrated his first marriage in Horton Bay's Congregational Church.

Stage two (5.7 miles) From Horton Bay it's downhill, when Boyne City Road curves to the right at 10.4 miles. You'll find paved shoulders on both sides of the road at 13.9 miles and then arrive at the entrance of Young State Park at 14.1 miles. The 563-acre park features 297 modern campsites in three camping areas along with 3 miles of hiking trails and a wide sandy beach in its day-use area. This is an alternative place to begin the tour, but if you plan to camp here reserve a site in advance. The campground is filled almost daily from early July to mid-August. The park is also an excellent place for that snack or lunch you packed as there is a grassy picnic area overlooking the beach and a concessionaire store. There is no fee for cyclists entering the park.

Boyne City limits is just down the road at 14.6 miles; after passing through a residential section the road curves sharply to the right into the downtown area at 15.4 miles. In town, the road is called Michigan Avenue and public restrooms will be passed to your right at 15.7 miles. Boyne City is a charming place on the lake with a distinct main street of shops, restaurants and lodging. For fine dining, try Stafford's One Water Street (616-582-3434), part of the Stafford chain, including Stafford's Bay View Inn and Stafford's Weathervane Restaurant in Charlevoix. Or try The Depot for an overall good meal.

Stage three (11 miles) From Boyne City, cycle on North Lake Street past Lake Charlevoix and the marina. Veterans Memorial Park is to the right at 16.6 miles where you'll find public restrooms nearby. Turn right on Main Street, which curves to the left and becomes Front Street still closely hugging the lakeshore. There's another public park to your right at 16.9 miles and then some gorgeous condominiums overlooking the lake before bike paths appear on the right hand side of the road at 17.4 miles. The road becomes North Division Street again as it follows the

The Ironton Ferry carries passengers across the South Arm.

lakeshore and then Lake Shore Drive.

A short but interesting side trip here is to ride to Avalanche Overlook Park for some of the best vistas in northwest Michigan. Just before Division Street turns into Lake Shore Road, turn left on Lake Street and then left on Ann Street. The park is a quarter mile at the end of Ann Street.

How steep is Avalanche Overlook? It's 473 steps and 11 rest benches to the top and was once a downhill ski slope. But from its lofty peak, you can see all of Boyne City, the length of Lake Charlevoix and the hills that surround it to the north. You can practically see this entire 35-mile bicycle tour.

Back on Lake Shore, there is not a lot of traffic, but the pavement can be a little rough before things smooth out at 18.5 miles. You'll cycle through the small village of Advance at 19.8 miles, where you'll find a grocery store on the corner and the road to East Jordan. Continue straight, following the lakeshore and soon a sign appears saying "Ironton Ferry is Open." Yeah!! As you look across the lake, you'll enjoy its hue of greenish blues, especially on a sunny day before a steep hill at 21.4 miles interrupts your daydreaming. At Whiting County Park the road swings away from the lake and becomes Ferry Road. Shift gears, climb another hill, which curves to the right at 23 miles, pass a golf course and a scattering of homes and you'll be rewarded at 26.4 miles with a long downhill stretch. Ferry Road ends at the Ironton Ferry (how appropriate!) at 26.8 miles. Time to cruise ahead of any cars waiting there and pay your 50 cents for the short 5-minute ride on one of the few cable-operated ferries in the United States.

Stage four (7.9 miles) From the ferry landing, the road curves to the right and travels up a steep hill and northwest towards Charlevoix on M-66. At 29.7 miles, you'll pass Castle Park, a popular spot for rock concerts, and then a wine cellar. M-66 features wide, paved shoulders on both sides beginning at 31.3 miles and at 32 miles it deadends into US-31. Turn right on US-31 for a short jaunt back to Charlevoix.

Civilization in the form of fast food is now in view. McDonald's will be to your right, and Pizza Hut to your left at 32.4 miles. In downtown Charlevoix, US-31 narrows to two lanes of traffic (called Bridge Street here), causing a major bottleneck for summer tourists. Be careful as you cycle through this stretch and pay attention to the possibilities for post-ride options: fine dining, maybe an art fair, or perhaps a scenic cruise. Hungry? Try Tom's Mom's for huge cookies, soups and sandwiches. You'll be back to your starting point at the VFW Hall at 34.7 miles.

Shorter option (12 miles) From Boyne City, head south following the lakeshore and then northwest along Lake Shore Drive. A little more than 6 miles, Whiting County Park is a perfect place to stop and rest before backtracking to your car.

Bicycle sales, service
Ace Hardware, 403 Bridge St., Charlevoix; (616) 547-4841.
High Gear, 1103 Old Tannery Creek, Petoskey; (616) 347-6118.

Bicycle repair

American Cycle, 100 N. Division Rd., Petoskey; (616) 347-6877.

Area attractions

Horton Bay General Store, Horton Bay; (616) 582-7827.

Ironton Ferry, Ironton; (616) 547-9036

Beaver Island Boat Co., Charlevoix; (616) 547-2311.

Bay Breeze Schooner Co., Charlevoix; (616) 547-0024.

Miss Charlevoix (Ward Brothers Cruises, Inc.), Charlevoix; (616) 547-2371.

Voyageur, Cruises Unlimited, Charlevoix; (616) 547-0188.

Pirates Cove Adventure Golf, Petoskey; (616) 347-1123.

Area events and festivals

May: Petunia Planting, Charlevoix

July: Venetian Festival, Charlevoix; Craft Show, Charlevoix; Annual Home Tour, Charlevoix; Fourth of July parade, Horton Bay.

August: Waterfront Art Fair & Castle Farm Art Show, Charlevoix; Sidewalk sales, Charlevoix.

October: Apple Fest, Charlevoix.

Travel information

Charlevoix Chamber of Commerce; (616) 547-2101.

Charlevoix Convention & Visitors Bureau; (800) 367-8557.

Boyne City Chamber of Commerce; (616) 582-6222.

Boyne Country Convention & Visitors Bureau; (800) 456-0197, (800) 845-2828 (in Michigan only) or (616) 348-2755.

Taking in the view of Lake Michigan from a bluff along M-119.

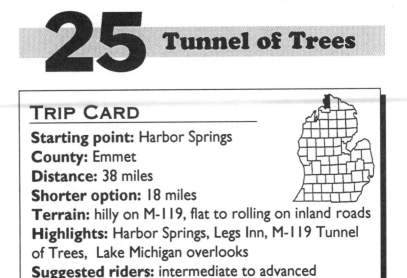

25 Tunnel of Trees

TRIP CARD

Starting point: Harbor Springs
County: Emmet
Distance: 38 miles
Shorter option: 18 miles
Terrain: hilly on M-119, flat to rolling on inland roads
Highlights: Harbor Springs, Legs Inn, M-119 Tunnel of Trees, Lake Michigan overlooks
Suggested riders: intermediate to advanced

National Geographic magazine once called M-119 one of the most beautiful drives in the country. Little wonder why. From Harbor Springs northward, the state highway follows the rugged Lake Michigan coastline but more times than not there is no view of the Great Lake whatsoever. The beauty of this narrow road is found in the trees shading the pavement, in the tunnels of trees you pass through and not the views you gaze upon.

Throughout this book, I've written about tunnels and canopies of trees. Indeed, Michigan is blessed with an abundance of species of hardwood trees, that form canopies that people from other states drool over (well, not literally). But here we could affectionately call the Cross Village route the "mother of all tunnels of trees." M-119 is the longest, the most rolling, and the greenest of all tunnels. You get the picture.

Perched high above the Lake Michigan shoreline, M-119 provides tantalizing glimpses of the lake, but mostly it's the roadside lined with trees and the hills that wind, dip and curve, that provide bicyclists with refreshing shade - even in the hottest of summer days. This tunnel of all tunnel of trees is the most northern route in the book, a route that ends at Cross Village before looping back.

The ride, which includes 21 miles on M-119, is a tour for experienced cyclists who want the thrill and fun of many ascents and descents. It will challenge and reward your cycle-worthy legs with naturally beautiful scenery, some of the best this region has to offer. Because this area of Emmet County is so devoid of towns and development, there is far less traffic on M-119 than on US-31, the highway most motorists usually take when travelling to Mackinaw City or the Upper Peninsula. The hills for the most part are manageable because of the momentum from the downhills.

Mention Cross Village to anyone who has been there and they think of one place - Legs Inn. If you can imagine it, Legs Inn (616-526-2281) is a place that combines a respect of the Indian culture, a Polish heritage and a love of northwest Michigan. It was built by Stanley Smolak, a Chicagoan, who fell in love with the area and moved to Cross Village in 1921. Smolak quickly made friends with the Ottawa Indians, who inducted him into their tribe as "Chief White Cloud." He built the Legs Inn of driftwood and stone he found along the shoreline with unique results. It's a historical landmark with Polish and American cuisine, including outdoor dining overlooking Lake Michigan. There are even lakeside, housekeeping cottages.

Today, Stanley Smolak's ancestors keep the tradition going. "It's weird, this place is weird," said one visitor to the Legs Inn. She was referring to the interior of the place, filled with pieces of driftwood in the shape of different sculptures. At the Legs Inn, they serve Polish entrees including pierogi (stuffed dumplings), gotabki (stuffed cabbage rolls) and bigos (a hearty stew). Plus you can enjoy imported Polish beers (try Krakus). This ethnic restaurant is a great stopover for cyclists - about halfway through the longer loop - before cycling back to the Harbor Springs area.

Harbor Springs, your starting point, is an affluent tourist town. Harbor Springs impresses visitors with its expensive Victorian

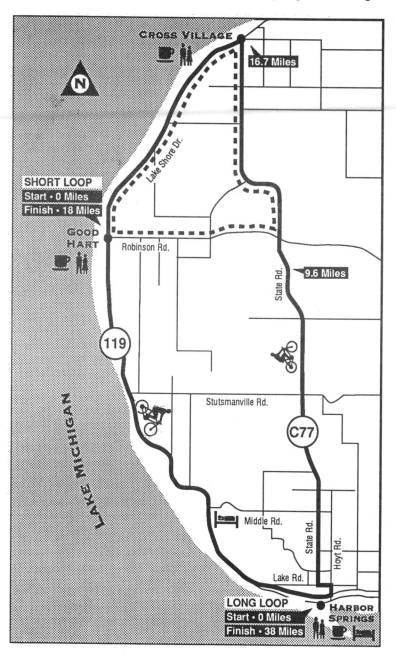

CROSS VILLAGE

16.7 Miles

Lake Shore Dr.

SHORT LOOP
Start • 0 Miles
Finish • 18 Miles

GOOD HART

Robinson Rd.

State Rd.

9.6 Miles

119

LAKE MICHIGAN

Stutsmanville Rd.

C77

Middle Rd.

State Rd.

Hoyt Rd.

Lake Rd.

LONG LOOP
Start • 0 Miles
Finish • 38 Miles

HARBOR SPRINGS

cottages and the view from "The Bluff" overlooking the water and the picturesque harbor. The business district of Harbor Springs is where you can find boutiques with the latest beachwear or other trendy, upscale clothing. Naturally, there are numerous restaurants. (Hey! Would we do a bike tour where there wasn't?) For ice cream, try Juilleret's (616-526-2821), the first soda shop in the area or Kilwin's (616-526-2802). For pizza, it's Turkey's Pizza (616-526-6041) or, for more of a dining experience, try The New York (616-526-6285) or Stafford's Pier (616-526-6201). As Harbor Springs is a resort town, casual attire (i.e. biking shorts) is acceptable at almost all restaurants.

Stage one (16.7 miles) From the south end of Harbor Springs on M-119, head right (north) on Hoyt Road. Then turn immediately to your left on Lake Road at a 2-way stop sign at 0.2 miles. Turn right on State Road, also called County Road 77, at almost 1 mile. State Road is a lightly travelled, inland road that heads north and in the beginning has gravel shoulders and some rolling hills and open farmland. At 2.1 miles there are paved shoulders on both sides. The road curves to the left and downhill at 3.4 miles followed by more curves and a long uphill stretch beginning at 8.9 miles.

A scenic, densely wooded area and a "Welcome to Readmond Township" sign greets you at 9.6 miles, and then it's a downhill to the right. Beginning at 11.4 miles, you encounter more hills as the road swings to the left, followed by more hills and more twists and more turns in CR-77 at 12.9 miles. This first stage is a long one - no place to stop for refreshments or a bathroom break - so be prepared!

The road narrows with no shoulders at 14 miles and then curves to your left as you enter Cross Village at 16.7 miles. Turn right on Lakeshore Drive and you will find yourself at the Legs Inn, a "must-stop" on your cycling itinerary. There's also the Cross Village General Store nearby.

But Legs Inn is definitely the attraction here. Outside the inn

Legs Inn, best Polish restaurant in Cross Village (and the only one!).

is bizarre at best; a building of boulders and wood, topped off by inverted stone legs (thus its name) and surrounded by a tipi, totem poles and a figurehead of an Indian chief. The interior is filled with Smolak's polished sculpture - more driftwood than any decent fire marshal would allow if Cross Village had one. The bar itself is one gigantic tree trunk while the doors are made entirely out of knots of wood that took Smolak more than two years to piece together. Don't linger here too long - you're still 21 miles from Harbor Springs.

Stage two (7.5 miles) Once you've experienced Legs Inn, it is time to begin your cycling adventure on the famous M-119. Head south and M-119 (also called Lake Shore) immediately curves to the right at 17.1 miles and then twists and curves and heads downhill. The shoulders along the road disappear at 17.4 miles and within a half mile you're winding uphill. It's okay because shortly you begin pedalling through the road's natural tunnels. This is a hilly stretch along a winding road and where the leafy tunnels end, you're rewarded with a view of Lake Michigan from the edge of a bluff. Spectacular country.

After passing an antique shop at 18.7 miles and climbing a long hill at 19.5 miles you re-enter Readmond Township. More curves and views of Lake Michigan are passed, along with the junction to Island View Road at 20.7 miles, followed by more tunnels that are spectacular in early October (though at that time of year the vehicle traffic tends to considerably heavier). There's a cemetery to the left at 21.9 miles and excellent views of Lake Michigan at 22.8 miles. You enter Good Hart at 24.2 miles, where you'll find an antique shop and the Good Hart Store (616-526-7661) which doubles up as a post office. The general store is open daily and has a deli with a selection of sandwiches, featuring homemade bread, as well as other items, if you didn't eat at the Legs Inn?

Stage three (14.1 miles) From Good Hart, keep cycling south on M-119 toward Harbor Springs. More tunnels are encountered as the road begins to wind downhill at 25.4 miles. You're rewarded with views of Lake Michigan along the way and an antique shop at 26.4 miles before challenged by more hills, including an especially steep one at 27.4 miles. You pass the junction to Stutsmanville Road at 28.6 miles and another nice view of the lake within a mile. M-119 continues to twist and curve its way south and you find you are cycling up then down hill after hill in working off your last meal while justifying another at the end of the tour.

You'll cycle by the site of a new housing development, signs that you're getting close to Harbor Springs, then coast down a long hill at 32.2 miles followed (naturally) by an uphill stretch. M-119 curves to the right at 32.7 miles, and then it's up another long hill where on your left is Birchwood Farm Estate at 34.1 miles followed by the Birchwood Inn (616-526-2151, 800-530-9955). The facilities include golf links, tennis courts, lodging and a restaurant. In the spring and fall, the Birchwood Inn sponsors bike tours along M-119.

You're not far from Harbor Springs now! A looooong downhill stretch is encountered at 37.1 miles and then you pass through a nice residential section in Harbor Springs. The road curves a couple of times to the right and finally you head downhill into Harbor Springs at 37.9 miles. Turn left at the 3-way stop at 38 miles.

If you have a sweet tooth, you will probably notice Kilwin's on the corner for homemade chocolates and ice cream. Antiques, art galleries, upscale clothing, a general store; you'll find it all in Harbor Springs! Turkey's Pizza, the best pizza in town, is on your right. You're back at the starting point on Hoyt Street at 38.5 miles! Congratulations- you've just completed the northernmost tour of our West Michigan region.

Shorter option (18 miles) Park at Good Hart store. Cycle east on Robinson Road to CR-77 (State Road); turn left (north). Stay on CR-77 into Cross Village. From Cross Village, cycle south on M-119 back to starting point in Good Hart.

Bicycle sales, service or rental
Touring Gear, 114 E. Third, Harbor Springs; (616) 526-7152.
High Gear, 11103 Old Tannery Creek, Petoskey; (616) 347-6118.
American Cycle, 100 N. Division, Petoskey; (616) 347-6877.
Area attractions
Legs Inn, Cross Village; (616) 526-2281.
Pirates Cove Adventure Golf, Petoskey; (616) 347-1123.
Gaslight District, downtown shopping area, Petoskey
Area events and festivals
May: Spring Shoreline Bike Tour, Birchwood Inn, Harbor Springs.
July: Fourth of July Parade & Fireworks, Petoskey & Harbor Springs; Harbor Springs Art Festival; Venetian Festival, Charlevoix.
September: Fall Shoreline Bike Tour, Birchwood Inn.
Travel information
Boyne Country Visitors Bureau; (800) 456-0197 (toll-free nationwide) or (800) 845-2828 (in Michigan) or (616) 348-2755.
Petoskey Regional Chamber of Commerce; (800) 456-0197 or (800) 845-2828 (in Michigan).

Cyclists pause in front of the Bicycle Museum in Three Oaks (bike tour number one).

Appendix

Accomodations

Lodging located on or near the routes listed with the corresponding bike tour number. Lodging listed below is just a sampling of the many choices in West Michigan.

Tour 3: Shady Shores Resort, 51256 Garret, Dowagiac, MI 49047; (616) 424-5251.

Tour 4: Boulevard Suite Hotel, 521 Lake Blvd., St. Joseph, MI 49085; (616) 983-6600.

Tour 5: The Christmere House, 110 Pleasant St., Sturgis, MI 49091; (616) 651-8303.

Tour 6: Kal-Haven Bed & Breakfast, 23491 Paulson Rd., Gobles, MI 49055; (616) 628-4932.

Tour 7: Maplewood Hotel, 428 Butler St., Saugatuck, MI 49453; (616) 857-1771.

Tour 8: Country Inn By Carlson, 12260 James St., Holland, MI 49424; (616) 396-6677.

Tour 9: Days Inn, 310 Pearl St. NW, Grand Rapids, MI 49504; (616) 235-7611.

Tour 12: Grandma's House Bed & Breakfast, 126 S. Fremont St., Rockford, MI 49341; (616)866-4111.

Tour 13: Michillinda Beach Lodge, 5207 Scenic Dr., Whitehall, MI 49461; (616) 893-1895.

Tour 14: Silver Sands Resort, RR 1 Box 318, Mears, MI 49436; (616) 873-3769.

Tour 15: Trail's End Lodge, 10233 Bus. US 31, Montague, MI 49437; (616) 894-4339.

Tour 16: Snyder's Shoreline Inn, 903 W. Ludington Ave., Ludington, MI 49431; (616) 845-1261.

Tour 17: Best Western Bill Oliver's Resort, M-55 West, P.O. Box 266, Cadillac, MI 49601; 1-800-OLIVER-5.

Tour 18: The Beach House, 221 Lake St., Beulah, MI 49617; (616) 882-5075.

Tour 19: The Narrows Motel & Dairy Bar, 6999 W. CR 616, Glen Arbor, MI 49636; (616) 334-4141.

Tour 20: The Jolli Lodge, M-22, Lake Leelanau, MI 49653; (616) 256-9291.

Tour 22: The Interlochen, 2275 M-137, P.O. Box 194 Interlochen, MI 49643; (616) 276-9221.

Tour 23: Torch Tip Resort, R. 1 Box 972-R, Kewadin, MI 49648; (616) 599-2313

Tour 24: Weathervane Terrace Hotel, 111 Pine River Lane, Charlevoix, MI 49720; (616) 547-9955; 1-800-552-0025.

Tour 25: Birchwood Inn, 7077 Lake Shore Dr., Harbor Springs, MI 49740; (616)526-2151 or 1-800-530-9955.

Additional information

West Michigan Tourist Association, 136 E. Fulton St., Grand Rapids, MI 49503; (616) 456-8557.

Michigan Travel Bureau, 333 S. Capitol Ave., Lansing, MI 48933; 1-800-5432-YES.

Michigan Department of Transportation, 425 W. Ottawa St., Lansing, MI 48909; (Send for order blank: individual Michigan county cycling maps available).

League of Michigan Bicyclists, P.O. Box #16201, Lansing, MI 48901; (616) 452-BIKE (free calendar of organized bike tours and cycling poster).

A cyclist stops at the Curious Kids Museum in St. Joseph.

Annual rides in West Michigan

May: Kal-Haven Trailblazer, Kalamazoo and South Haven; Harbor Springs Cycling Classic (May and September).

June: The 100 Grand, Grand Rapids; Clean Air Ride, Grand Rapids; Flag Day Festival Mountain Bike Tour, Three Oaks; Crystal Lake Tour, Frankfort; Michigan National 24-Hour Challenge, Byron Center; Pedal Across Lower Michigan (PALM), South Haven; Michigan MS 150 Bike Tour, Grand Rapids.

July: Holland Hundred; Ride Around Torch Lake (RAT), Elk Rapids; Coast to Coast Tour, southwestern Michigan.

August: Shoreline Bicycle Tour, New Buffalo; Heritage Tour, Kingsley.

September: Leelanau Lakeshore Loop, Suttons Bay; One Day Ride Across Michigan, Muskegon; Vineyard Classic Bicycle Tour, Paw Paw; Cereal City Century, Battle Creek; Leelanau Harvest Tour, Cedar; Apple Cider Century, Three Oaks.

October: Octoberfest, Whitehall; Turning Leaves Century, Edwardsburg.

West Michigan cycling clubs

Battle Creek Bicycle Club, c/o Kellogg Community College, 450 North Ave., Battle Creek, MI 49015.

Brickheads, 430 W. 14th St., Traverse City, MI 49684.

Cherry Capital Cycling Club, P.O. Box 1807, Traverse City, MI 49684.

Glen Lake Bicycle Club, Attn: Ivan Ford, Glen Lake High School, Rt. 2, Maple City, MI 49664.

Harbor Springs Bicycle Club, 114 E. Third St., Harbor Springs, MI 49740.

Kalamazoo Bicycle Club; 1215 Woodland, Kalamazoo, MI 49002.

Michigan Human Powered Vehicle Association, 2708 Lake Shore Dr. Apt. 307, St. Joseph, MI 49085

Waiting for the Saugatuck chain ferry.

Muskegon Bicycle Club, Box 922, Muskegon, MI 49443.

Rapid Wheelman, P.O. Box 1008, Grand Rapids, MI 49501.

Three Oaks Spokes Bicycle Club, 110 N. Elm St., Three Oaks, MI 49128.

Thornapple Valley Bikers, P.O. Box 115, Hastings, MI 49058.

Tulip City Two-Wheelers, P.O. Box 2304, Holland, MI 49423.

West Michigan Spokes Folks, 1790 Roberts, Muskegon, MI 49442.

Wheel People of St. Joseph, 1303 E. Chicago Rd., Sturgis, MI 49091.

 Michgian Rails-To-Trails

The Rails-To-Trails Movement

A system of interconnecting pathways linking Michigan together is the vision of the Rails-to-Trails Conservancy of Michigan.

The movement has taken hold. There are 50 rail trails in Michigan ranging from less than a mile to a 45-mile snowmobile trail in the Upper Peninsula. The map on page 221 depicting the existing trails, projects in the works and proposed trails is evidence that the Rails-to-Trails Conservancy's vision may one day be a reality. Slowly--inch by inch, foot by foot, mile by mile, Michigan is preserving its railroad heritage by converting abandoned railroad corridors to recreational trails for all ages of cyclists, hikers, horseback riders and in-line skaters.

West Michigan has a substantial number of proposed trails and three of the major existing routes, also described in this book. Each of the existing trails has a unique story of how they began, but all became a reality because of collaborating interests and solid working relationships (sometimes unprecedented) between municipalities, trail user groups and the generosity and understanding of adjoining landowners.

The Hart-Montague Trail State Park Michigan's first linear state park winds more than 22 miles through the countryside of Oceana and northern Muskegon counties. Bill Field, a private citizen and rail trail advocate purchased the corridor and gifted it to the state. In its first few months of operation in 1989, an

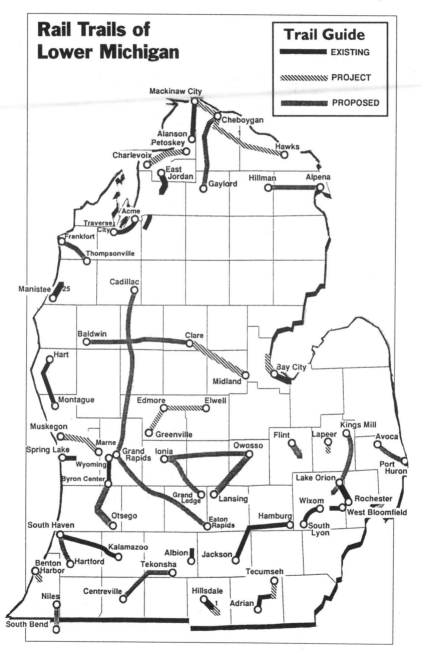

Rail Trails of Lower Michigan

Trail Guide

EXISTING

PROJECT

PROPOSED

Mackinaw City

Cheboygan

Alanson
Petoskey

Charlevoix

East Jordan

Gaylord

Hillman

Hawks

Alpena

Acme

Traverse City

Frankfort

Thompsonville

Cadillac

Manistee 25

Baldwin

Clare

Midland

Bay City

Hart

Montague

Edmore

Elwell

Muskegon

Greenville

Kings Mill

Spring Lake

Marne

Grand Rapids

Ionia

Owosso

Flint

Lapeer

Avoca

Wyoming

Byron Center

Port Huron

Lake Orion

Grand Ledge

Lansing

Wixom

Rochester

West Bloomfield

Otsego

Eaton Rapids

Hamburg

South Haven

South Lyon

Kalamazoo

Albion

Jackson

Benton Harbor

Hartford

Tekonsha

Tecumseh

Centreville

Hillsdale 1

Adrian

Niles

South Bend

estimated 45,000 recreationists used the trail. The north half of the trail was paved in 1989 and the southern half completed in 1990.

A Michigan National Resources Trust Fund (MNRTF) grant assisted the development and the remaining mileage was completed using Department of Natural Resources (DNR) Recreation Improvement Fund (RIF). The trail is managed by the DNR Parks Division as a linear state park. Individual and family permits are required which helps defray operational costs.

Kal-Haven Trail Sesquicentennial State Park After years of negotiation, the DNR purchased this 34-mile corridor that traverses woods and countryside, using MNRTF funds. The surfacing of the trail (crushed screen limestone and crushed screened cinder slag) began in 1990. Individual and family permits are also required on this trail.

Monies for trail improvements come from two DNR funds and the Michigan Department of Transportation non-motorized transportation fund. The "Friends of the Kal-Haven Trail" provide additional funding and labor for trail improvement and operation.

Kent Trails With DNR grant assistance, this non-motorized 15-mile corridor that runs from near downtown Grand Rapids to Byron Center, opened in 1992. It includes 6 miles of rail corridor, road sections and paths over a new pipeline. Six governmental bodies help maintain the popular trail, recognized statewide for its contribution to recreation.

Traverse Area Recreation Trail The T.A.R.T., primarily an 8-foot wide asphalt path, will extend across the greater Grand Traverse region from the West Bay in Traverse City to Acme near the Grand Traverse Resort. Just under 3 miles of the trail is currently paved (1993) near the West Bay in Traverse City. Some of the trail, owned by the Michigan Department of Transportation, parallels existing rail trail. Financial support comes from local charities, Grand Traverse County and Friends of T.A.R.T. The trail

The trail will eventually include scenic overlooks and rest stops.

For more information Cyclists who wish to get involved in the development and planning of Michigan's Rails-to-Trails program should contact the state chapter of the National Rails-To-Trails Conservancy:

Rails-to-Trails Conservancy of Michigan
913 W. Holmes, Suite 227-D
Lansing, MI 48910
Telephone: (517) 393-6022

The Author

Karen Gentry, a resident of Grand Rapids, Mich., is currently a reporter for a West Michigan newspaper. She formerly worked for the West Michigan Tourist Association, where she was the project coordinator for the first Lake Michigan Circle Tour Guide. She was also the editor of Trails-a-Way, a regional camping publication and a high school English and journalism teacher.

Gentry is a journalism graduate of Central Michigan University and a graduate of Lake Michigan Catholic High School in St. Joseph, Mich. Besides cycling, she enjoys other outdoor pursuits such as running and cross country skiing.